HENRY FORD

HENRY FORD

by
CY CALDWELL

illustrated by
EDD ASHE

THE BODLEY HEAD
LONDON

First Published 1955

Printed in Great Britain by
WESTERN PRINTING SERVICES LTD, BRISTOL
for JOHN LANE THE BODLEY HEAD LTD
28 Little Russell Street, London, W.C.1

To My Son Alan

LIST OF ILLUSTRATIONS

MEN OF THE MODERN AGE

A biographical series dealing with outstanding men of courage, drive and initiative who, over the past two centuries, have made their mark, each in his different sphere, on our modern age. The subjects of the first five titles will indicate the nature and the wide range of this new series, which is intended principally for the child of twelve years and over.

Chapter One

HENRY FORD was born on his father's farm at Dearborn on the rainy afternoon of July 30, 1863. That was a memorable month in American history, for it marked the turning point in the war between the States. On July 3 the battle of Gettysburg in Pennsylvania had closed with the defeat of General Robert E. Lee's army; and a day later the Confederate garrison of thirty-seven thousand men had surrendered at Vicksburg on the banks of the Mississippi.

In these modern times when the air-line passenger may eat dinner in New York and breakfast in San Francisco, it takes a little imagination to picture what life in the United States was like when Henry Ford was born. In the sixties, the only comfortable way to travel between New York and the West Coast was by clipper ship or almost equally leisurely steamship, around Cape Horn and all of South America; or the passenger could land at Panama, cross the Isthmus by railroad, and embark at Balboa on another ship for the journey up the Coast.

It was not until 1869, when Henry was six years old, that the Union Pacific Railroad, built from the Missouri River at Omaha, met the Central Pacific, which had been built eastward from San Francisco. Its rails and all equipment, including wood-burning steam locomotives and railroad cars, were brought around Cape Horn by sailing ships and steamships.

Before the historic meeting of the first two trains, at a point fifty-three miles west of Ogden, Utah, on May 10, 1869, the traveller who wished to cross the continent overland went by rail as far as Council Bluffs, Iowa, or St. Joseph, Missouri, and then continued his journey by stagecoach or pack train.

It was an exhausting journey for the passenger, and also for his pocketbook: from Kansas to California the fare was five hundred dollars, and the hardy traveller paid for his own food and lodging en route.

Railroad travel in the sixties was far from comfortable. In winter the cars were heated by a stove at one end of the car. On a cold day one might encounter many varying degrees of temperature, from tropical heat near the stove to arctic cold at the other end of the car. Thoughtful travellers tried to sit near the middle, not only for warmth, but to be as far as possible from the wheels, which were so poorly sprung that the ends of the car jumped up and down, while the centre of the car merely swayed with an easier motion.

No matter where one sat, draughts came whistling in around the windows, whose wood frames were so loose in winter that cinders came in with the draughts, so tight in hot or rainy weather that one couldn't open them.

It was not until 1867, four years after Henry Ford was born, that George Pullman built the first Pullman Palace sleeping car and sent it trundling over the rails to usher in a new era of travel luxury.

In the sixties there were no paved roads anywhere outside the limits of cities and the larger towns. Only main streets were paved, usually with cobblestones, and passengers riding in omnibuses and coaches whose wheels were rimmed with tyres of solid iron were well shaken up. Pneumatic rubber tyres were not to make their welcome appearance until the bicycle era of the so-called "Gay Nineties". The nineties, it may be said, were gay only by comparison with the eighties and seventies, which were positively glum.

The streets of cities and the homes of their inhabitants were lighted by illuminating gas or kerosene oil lamps. The electric light bulb was not to be invented until 1879 by Thomas A. Edison, who was sixteen years of age and working as a telegraph operator when Henry Ford was born.

In the sixties, transportation within the larger cities was by horse-drawn carriage or omnibus—which today we call simply a bus—or by horse-drawn streetcars on rails. The electric street-car did not make its appearance until 1885 when Henry Ford was a young man of twenty-two.

The United States west of the Mississippi was almost unpopulated, except for areas near rivers or main routes of through travel. From Minnesota to the Gulf of Mexico still was largely frontier America.

No more than four million people lived in that tremendous area and the majority of these had settled in small communities along rivers, or had moved on to California in the great rush for gold that started in 1849.

In what is now the great wheat belt of America, Indians, trappers, and a few travellers roamed the prairies swarming with immense herds of buffaloes. Their meat was good eating and their hides, tanned with the hair left on, were popular for carriage robes. These two factors practically guaranteed the speedy extinction of the buffalo.

The West was untamed when Henry Ford was a boy; and many of the hardy settlers were as shaggy as the buffaloes they hunted. Civilization was being carried to the expectant Indians by means of the rifle, bad whisky, and shoddy trade goods. The result was war.

The year after Henry Ford was born, the Cheyenne warriors attacked a coach line east of Denver and killed several persons who were on their way to relieve the Indians of the last of their hunting grounds. Four years later these same Cheyennes, stubbornly resisting all attempts to civilize them out of existence, swept through western Kansas, spreading death and desolation among the settlers. The United States Army then took the field, and soon the whole frontier from Minnesota to Kansas was ablaze. The Indian wars continued for a dozen years.

When Henry Ford was a boy he must have heard his parents and the neighbours talking about the Indian raids on many a night when the wind whistled around the Dearborn farmhouse, while Henry and his brothers and sisters huddled around the fire in the big kitchen, imagining Indians creeping upon them from the surrounding woods.

Such was the America of the sixties when Henry Ford was a boy. How he came to be born in Dearborn, Michigan, instead of in Ireland where the Ford family had lived for centuries, suggests a brief glance at the Ford family and William Ford, Henry's father.

Chapter Two

WILLIAM FORD was born in the city of Cork, Southern Ireland, in 1827 and was raised as a farmer. By the time he was twenty, things were in a very bad way in Ireland.

In 1844 the potato blight made its first appearance in North America, was carried across the Atlantic, supposedly in shipments of diseased potatoes, reached Europe, and attacked the potato crops of Belgium, Germany, Holland, and Ireland. In a few weeks' time the abundant Irish potato crop—then a main staple of Irish diet—became a waste of putrefying vegetation. Scarcely a bushel of whole potatoes was taken from the ground.

In addition to absentee English landlords, who had held their Irish tenants in virtual peonage ever since Oliver Cromwell's day, the unfortunate Irish now were faced with an even greater disaster: crop failure. From 1845 to 1851 nearly a million Irish men, women, and children died of starvation. And in the decade that followed this disaster more than a million and a half Irish people emigrated to America. Some came seeking political freedom; but all came looking for something to eat.

Young William Ford, Henry's father, was one of these emigrants, a sturdy, resolute young Irish farmer, willing to work

13

at any job he could find. He went to Michigan and worked on an arsenal that was being built near Detroit. After that he was a tracklayer on a railroad, and worked at various odd jobs, including that of farm hand. He worked hard from dawn to dusk, was careful of his money, and within a few years had saved enough to buy a farm of forty acres in Dearborn Township, nine miles from Detroit. On his farm he built a two-storey frame house containing four rooms, to which a few years later he added two more rooms.

In 1862, when he was thirty-five years of age and a successful farmer, William Ford married Mary Litogot, adopted daughter of Patrick O'Hearn, from whom William had bought his forty acres. Mary then was about eighteen years old, a dark-haired lovely girl of Dutch and Scandinavian ancestry. She was cheerful and serene, which was indeed fortunate for her, as a woman's life on a farm in those days was no picnic. Farm life meant work.

The farmer's wife had to cook big nourishing meals, not only for her family but also for several extra hired hands during harvest season. She did all the family washing, scrubbing it by hand on a washboard while bending over a tub of steaming water and soapsuds. The soap she made herself from fat and lye. It was a powerful compound, guaranteed to remove dirt from the clothes—along with some skin from the hands of the operator.

Henry Ford recalls how hard his mother worked, and how cheerful she always was. The washing would be hung out, sometimes in below zero weather, and, when it was dry, or frozen stiff as a board, taken in to be ironed. She would wash on Monday, iron on Tuesday—or even Monday night it if chanced to be a large wash that week. Most farmers' wives began the week with what came to be called "a crick in the back".

By Wednesday, however, this crick would disappear, driven away by the healthy exercise attendant upon kneading dough and mixing the ingredients for cakes and rolling out piecrust; for there was home baking at least once and usually twice a week. There was no baker's shop to run to, no friendly baker's delivery man rolling up to the door in a truck loaded with bread, cakes, pies. If a woman wanted those things for her family, she baked them herself, thanked God for the ingredients, and cheerfully threw in her labour as a matter of course.

She also had to can fruits and vegetables in season, make jams, preserves, jellies, and help her husband or the boys smoke hams and bacon. In her spare time she did the family sewing, making most of the children's clothes herself, and sometimes spinning the yarn and weaving the cloth as well.

As the children came along, she naturally looked after them, usually without the assistance of a hired girl, who was an unknown luxury on many farms. A farmer's wife expected to work, and her expectations always were realized in fullest measure.

Compared to some other farmers' wives in the neighbourhood, Mrs. Ford got off easily. They didn't have to smoke their own meat, but bought it from a neighbour; and Mrs. Ford didn't have to weave cloth, although sometimes she did, just for the sheer joy of it—in spare moments.

As the children came—and she had six including Henry—she made all their clothes. That was in her spare time, of course, when she wasn't washing or ironing, cleaning the house or cooking meals for the family and the hired hands, or putting up preserves, or canning fruit or feeding the chickens. It was restful to be able occasionally to sit down for a spell in the nice warm kitchen, with nothing to do but rock gently back and forth in the old horsehair-covered rocker, and make clothes for six children, and mend the clothes that were wearing out, and darn the socks and sew on buttons.

Henry's father raised corn, wheat, oats, buckwheat, potatoes, onions, beets, turnips, carrots and the usual garden vegetables. There was an orchard of apple, pear, peach, and cherry trees that grew fruit with a delicious flavour that Henry Ford never was able to find when he became a man—although he then owned that same orchard with some of the trees still bearing fine fruit.

There was a wooded area on the place from which William Ford cut timber and wood for fuel; and there was a pasture in which he kept a dozen or more cows, using the milk mainly to make butter, a profitable source of farm income. He also kept from fifteen to thirty hogs, feeding them on corn and skim milk and selling them in the Detroit market when they were fattened.

On an American farm of the sixties, children were a potential source of income, practically another—and livelier—farm crop. When the boys were old enough to feed the chickens or herd the cows or do a little hoeing in the vegetable garden—say around six or seven years old—they were given their chores to do, and thus learned at an early age that life was not exactly a bowl of cherries. By practical experience they learned that the earth did not present them with a living on a silver platter. Everything they ate had to be pried from the rich soil by means of labour: their father's, the hired man's, and their own.

It was healthy work in the fresh air, guaranteed to develop muscles and add to the family income. As a side line it also developed character and turned out a citizen who accepted hard work as casually as he accepted the sunshine and the rain. It is not an accident that many boys raised on an old-time American farm went to the city and became prominent in business or the professions. They had the necessary ingredients of stamina and character to start with.

Chapter Three

WHEN Henry was four years old, his father bought an additional forty acres; and later on he bought one hundred and fifty acres adjoining his farm in Springwell Township. As the years went by, Mr. Ford gradually built up one of the finest farms in the district.

At some little distance from the house were the barn, the corncrib, chicken house, implement shed, and other small buildings. There were fine large shade trees around the house and, a little distance away, the orchard. Part of the farm was in woodland: elm, hickory, beech, and walnut trees, with a scattering of maple, oak, and ash trees.

Rhulo Creek, shallow and willow bordered, wandered through the farm as though anxious to explore as many parts of it as possible, and was in no hurry to empty its waters into the nearby Rouge River, except in the spring, when it seemed to grow ambitious of becoming a river itself, and flooded the lower pastures where in summer the cows stood knee-deep in the lush grass.

One of Henry's first duties on the farm was to bring home

the cows in the evening, and drive them out to pasture after their milking at dawn. It was fun to do this in summer when the early morning sun raised curtains of mist from the lowlands, but not so much fun in the chill days of autumn or early spring when the air had a bite to it and a sleepy boy, without his breakfast, plodded along reluctantly, wishing he was back in a warm bed.

The horses, cows, hogs, chickens—all were interesting to the growing boy. They were more than stock for him to help his father look after; they were individuals with distinct personalities of their own, with good or not so good dispositions, and with as many varied peculiarities as human beings. Like all observant farm boys, Henry Ford acquired a knowledge of life from his surroundings.

Of special interest to him were the birds that made their nests and raised their families in the woodlands. One of his earliest recollections was of his father's taking him, when he was only three years old, to see a bird's nest in an old tree. He grew to know the birds well and to love them for the note of cheer they brought to the lonely farm: the chickadees, the bluebirds, the bobolinks, the Baltimore orioles, the meadow larks, scarlet tanagers, and the song sparrows. Their presence was encouraged, for they helped to control insect pests and they were a farmer's most able assistants in his constant battle with the natural enemies of agriculture.

There were a great many snakes around the farm—black snakes and blue racers and grass snakes. Henry, like most farm boys of those days, thought that all snakes were poisonous and therefore to be avoided. When he went barefoot in summer, these harmless farm dwellers added a spice of danger and adventure—imaginary though it was—that helped to make life more interesting for the boy.

Two years after Henry was born, the Fords had another son, John; and then at two-year intervals came two daughters, Margaret and Jennie; then two more sons, who were named William and Robert.

A large family in those days was an asset, like money in the bank. Better, in fact, for banks sometimes failed, and the entire investment was lost. Children, on the other hand, not only were a source of interest to their fond parents, but supplied much of their own keep.

As the older children took their places in the farm work, they did their share to raise the extra food needed to feed the younger ones. So whether a man raised a family of twelve or fifteen children or only two or three, he didn't have to work any harder. This possibly may explain why large families were so popular in farming communities.

The girls, of course, helped their mother in the house the very moment they could clutch a dish and dry it without dropping it on the kitchen floor. They started, as a rule, with the pot covers, metal and unbreakable, and in time graduated to china dishes. By the time they were ten they could be trusted with the company dinner set that made its appearance only on special occasions.

The girls learned to sew, to dust, to sweep, to help with the family washing, baking, and cooking. By the time she was twelve, any normally bright farm girl of the sixties could run a house all by herself—and often was forced to do so if the mother died.

Henry Ford's earliest recollections were of the big kitchen which served also as dining-room and living-room. Why heat extra rooms, when you can sit in only one room at a time? There was a wide fireplace and a crane from which cooking pots were suspended over the wood fire. The day when the picturesque fireplace was supplemented by a more utilitarian cooking stove marked a turning point in the fortunes of the Ford family: the intrusion of a bought iron stove that made the old fireplace built by Henry's father seem very antiquated indeed. His mother, however, never was heard to express any regrets that she no longer had to bend over an open fire and at times get smoke in her eyes when the wind was in a certain direction and blew smoke back down the chimney.

Watching his mother toiling at the stove, Henry once asked, "Mother, don't you ever get tired?"

"I have no time even to think of it," she said. "If you are busy enough, Henry, and interested in what you are doing, it won't occur to you to think of being tired until you drop into bed. And then you'll be so tired that before you have time to think about how tired you are, you will be asleep."

Later in his life, when he was working sixteen hours a day to perfect his first automobile, Henry Ford sometimes thought of his mother's words, and recognized the truth of them. He never minded hard work, perhaps because he had been raised with it, and recognized it as a constant companion of his boyhood: work from dawn to dark.

However, Henry was too sensible to love work for its own sake; he merely accepted it as a necessity of life. In his biography he says:

> My earliest recollection is that, considering the results, there was too much work on the place. That is the way I still feel about farming. . . . There was too much hand labour on our own and all other farms of the time. Even when very young I suspected that much might somehow be done in a better way. That is what took me into mechanics—although my mother always said that I was a born mechanic.

To his parents, Henry seemed to be just another hard-working, willing youngster. But that he could arrive at such a sound conclusion is evidence that he was wise beyond his years. The advance of civilization has been a retreat from hand labour —and Henry Ford recognized that fact early in his career.

Chapter Four

WHEN Henry was seven and a half years old he started
school. January 11, 1871, marked the beginning of his
formal education. Not that schooling in the seventies was attended by much formality in the Scotch Settlement School, a
small building with only one room and one teacher who wrestled
with the education of children from the first to the eighth grades.

The schoolhouse was painted red, as were most of the country
schools of that day; not because red was considered educational
or even beautiful, but simply because the basis of that paint is
red lead, a pigment possessing excellent covering power and
permanence. The taxpayers didn't want to paint the schoolhouse more frequently than they had to, so thrift chose the
colour of the educational institutions of the seventies.

This one-room little red schoolhouse was heated by a single
wood-burning stove attended by the larger boys, who took turns
bringing in wood from the pile of cordwood stacked against a
wall of the building. The teacher had little difficulty in main-
taining order, for instead of "keeping in" after school any un-
ruly youth, the teacher merely smiled and said, "William, you
will be here at seven o'clock tomorrow morning to start the fire.
The labour of starting it, and of trying to keep yourself warm

in the chill of early morning, will be a useful lesson in self-discipline.''

When Henry entered school the teacher was John Brainerd Chapman, a good and patient man for whom young Henry formed an abiding respect and affection. It had to be gradual, for it is normal in boys to meet their teacher with a certain guarded reserve, amounting at times to actual hostility.

Henry, however, was not averse to learning; so he looked upon his teacher as his friend. This alone set him apart as an unusual boy. Among Henry's later teachers was the father of Alonzo Bush, a school friend of Henry's, who also became a builder of automobiles. Henry remained friends for life with Mr. Chapman and Mr. Bush, firm in the belief that they had helped him, as undoubtedly they had.

Henry was a quiet boy and did his schoolwork with the same energy and devotion to duty that he displayed later in life when he built automobiles. Although whippings were usual, with a stout leather strap or a cane applied to a well-cushioned part of the anatomy, Henry never received one—which again is somewhat remarkable in a day when it was considered necessary to pound education into reluctant students.

Although he always behaved himself, and thus escaped minor disasters, Henry was never considered a teacher's pet. He went to school earnestly, determined to get an education, offering no resistance to whatever information was being imparted to him. And what he got, he held on to tenaciously, for his memory was remarkable.

The chief book in Henry's school was Webster's Elementary Spelling Book, called the Blue-back Speller because it was bound in blue cloth. But it was a fortunate choice of colours, for the book's outlook on life was unmistakably blue. It was packed from cover to cover with good advice and doleful proverbs and sayings full of horse sense—it being admitted everywhere that horses have more sense than humans.

In later years, when Henry Ford was asked by newspaper reporters to say a few words about some problem that was pressing upon the world, he would smile serenely and launch into a pronouncement taken straight from the source—that Blue-back Speller. There never was any doubt about what Henry meant, for his thoughts were clothed in simple words, none more than five or six letters long.

Another series of books that influenced young Henry Ford were the McGuffey Readers—a combined course of reading, spelling, history, and moral philosophy.

Never once in his pages did the good McGuffey question the existing order. The world, as McGuffey viewed it, was an eminently moral and highly satisfactory globe, where the key to success was to be honest, industrious, honour your parents, go to church, and help old ladies across the street. Eventually, one might become President.

McGuffey usually began his pages with a few words to be spelled and defined. Then he threw in a selection from the works of some writer known to lead a good moral life. There invariably was a moral in the selection, so the eager student could get himself a moral a day if he was attentive, and could take it.

Henry Ford, brought up on McGuffey, accepted his teachings without reservations, and remembered them. Through the years to come, when asked his opinion about this or that, he would answer in words that stemmed directly from the old master. Henry never let a moral get away from him.

Early in his school life, Henry Ford displayed indications of the qualities of leadership and initiative that he developed to such an amazing degree as the years passed.

Near the school was a small creek on the banks of which the boys often played during recess. The creek, in its unfettered course towards the Rouge River, seemed to offer a challenge to Henry, who had spent much of his young life battling Nature to help his father get a crop from the soil, despite such natural enemies of the farmer as weeds, insects, and other hazards of agriculture. Nature, to Henry, was something that any sensible person induced to help him usefully.

"Why not dam this creek, and set it to turning a water wheel?" he suggested to his playmates. The boys leaped at the suggestion, as in later years grown men leaped at others advanced by Henry Ford. The reasons for this were plain. Even as a boy, Henry was a quiet, thoughtful fellow whose ideas usually had something to do with a practical matter, such as making or building something.

The other boys set to with enthusiasm and built a fairly substantial rock dam across the creek, then filled it in with turf and clay. Henry, thus early displaying true executive ability, left the others to this necessary but back-tiring task, while he attended to the more brain-taxing matter of building a water wheel.

Under Henry's direction—he was too busy supervising to do any of the hard labour of course—the other boys built a millrace where Henry set his wheel when the water had risen high enough in the dam. Naturally, everything worked, which surprised nobody, for even as a boy Henry was known as one who could make things work.

This incident of the dam also taught Henry something about Nature's law of action and reaction—that whenever he did anything there always were after-effects. It was a lesson he never forgot.

By the time the water had risen high enough to fill the dam, it also had backed up far enough from the dam to flood several acres of potatoes and other crops growing along the creek.

The budding water-power tycoon soon learned to his discomfiture that to develop water power without having an irate farmer chase you with the avowed intention of collecting damages from your hide, it was advisable first to arrange for ownership of the land to be flooded.

Henry and his willing workers were ordered by the schoolmaster to demolish their dam and, as there were no early morning fires to light in springtime, they were kept in after school for a long time and were forced to read McGuffey's ideas about property rights. Henry learned so well that eventually he was able to own all the land and water rights in that vicinity, and thus have the right to build dams all over the place if he wanted —which, as it turned out, he did, to produce hydro-electric power not only for his huge River Rouge plant but for his farm at Dearborn as well.

As his school days went on, year after year, Henry took a larger and larger part in the work on his father's farm. He did all the chores that normally fell to the lot of a small boy on a farm where everybody worked. He took hard labour as a matter of course.

In the winter he spent most of his time at school, but as he grew older his chores were passed along to his younger brothers, and Henry took on a greater share of the farm work. By the time he was twelve, he was ploughing and doing a man's work. Few men, indeed, could plough a straighter furrow, nor follow the plough for longer hours.

The family was up at dawn, or a little before dawn. They went to bed at nine, for two good reasons: because they were dog-tired, and to save oil for the lamps, for oil was expensive.

Henry got up at daybreak in summer and before dawn in winter. But he was too intelligent to take any great amount of pleasure in the work. It was, he felt, too unrewarding for the effort expended; too much of doing the same monotonous thing over and over again, with not very much to show for it.

There was the task of getting water, for one thing. At first it was drawn from a well by a bucket suspended on a rope. And anyone who has drawn up dozens of buckets each day, and every day, to water the stock and to supply a large family's needs will agree with young Henry Ford that it was an uninspiring and wearing task. Even when his father installed a pump, it had to be pumped by hand, and the water had to be carried in buckets to the desired destination.

Henry felt that something should be done to lighten this back-breaking labour—for in nearby Detroit water flowed from taps. Why, he thought, should country dwellers be content for ever to carry water? Water would run to wherever you wanted it if only you provided the necessary arrangements. Even the early Romans who lived two thousand years ago, he learned in school, had water that flowed by gravity from many miles away. Surely modern Michigan should not be more backward than the Rome of twenty centuries ago. It was a logical thought, but rather surprising in a boy of twelve.

It must not be thought that Henry Ford was a lazy boy. He wasn't. He was intelligent enough to realize that back-tiring labour received a small reward and that its results were not commensurate with the energy expended. For instance, Henry never objected to driving a mowing machine, which he could sit on while a team of horses did the heavy work. But he never cared for hoeing corn, for he had to stand on his feet, walk along the rows, and lean over and move his arms vigorously.

In many respects, Henry was just an average American country boy. At school he did his work well. His teachers said that he was studious but apparently quite unimaginative.

His reading was confined largely to biography, which usually proves tough going for a boy. But Henry gulped down a life of Socrates and many others, among them Washington, Lincoln, and Grant. He never cared for history or fiction.

Henry was an active and play-loving boy; yet as soon as his school days were finished, he lost all interest in play or in sports. Although he had detested the work of the farm, a new and different kind of labour of hand and mind became recreation to Henry Ford. He toiled for long hours in his workshop, which was a joy and a never-ending interest.

As a boy Henry loved to go barefoot in summer. He hated to dress up on Sundays, in a white shirt and collar, the blue suit and laced shoes that were standard equipment for boys on churchgoing days.

The family went regularly to the Episcopal church and were devout members. Henry shared only passively in these activities and took church, as he took the weather, as something that he could do very little about.

He was a child of independent thought, but outwardly a conformist. He had his own way of thinking about things, but he never got into trouble by protesting too vigorously about anything.

He loved swimming, fishing, and roaming the fields studying the wild life of the district. He was friendly and liked to be with other boys. They played all the games of those days before baseball had been invented, such as prisoner's base, fox and geese, leap-frog, snap the whip. In season, he played marbles and flew kites, went in for foot races and jumping matches and wrestling. In the autumn, he went into the woods with the other boys and roamed far, gathering walnuts, hickory nuts, beechnuts and butternuts.

His father gave him a single-barrelled muzzle-loading shotgun, so he went hunting every autumn. There were rabbits, squirrels, partridges and quail in the surrounding woods and fields. Ducks and geese by the thousand paused briefly to feed in the marshes on their way to their winter quarters down south.

Henry became a good shot and liked the sport when he was a boy, but as a young man he lost his taste for hunting. Soon the killing of any wild animal or bird became impossible for him—an attitude that was reflected later on in his life, when he so vigorously expressed his feelings about war and the killing of human beings.

Henry had only a few pets. Sometimes he set a box trap for a squirrel, tamed it and kept it a while, then let it go free. Towards the end of his school years he had a small dog named Watch that accompanied him on long walks through the woods and fields. Henry became fond of the dog, and after it died he felt its loss keenly. He never had another dog.

In winter there was little work on the farm—except for caring for the animals, mending fences and farm equipment, cutting wood for the next winter. So there was ample time for winter sports such as sleighing and skating. Henry became an expert skater and would skate down frozen Rhulo Creek to the Rouge River, along it to the Detroit River, and sometimes as far up that river as Belle Isle, past the city of Detroit. Often the boys played shinty, from which modern hockey derives.

They were happy years for young Henry until he was twelve, when his mother died. Mrs. Ford had been more than a mother to her children. She had been their friend and patient, understanding counsellor. About her kindly little figure the whole life of the house had centred. Her quick, clever fingers had made the very clothes that all of them wore; her cheerful smile had made the darkest day seem bright with kindliness and love. Her loss was a cruel blow to the sensitive Henry, and he said afterwards, "The house was like a watch without a mainspring".

A married cousin of the family, a Mrs. Flaherty, came in to look after the children until Margaret Ford, entering her teens, undertook the care of the household. It was no light task, even for a grown woman, but Henry's slim, pretty young sister looked after the housekeeping and the younger children, did the cooking, sewed and even made clothes as her mother had done before her. The younger children helped as they could, and the life of the Ford home and farm went along, but never again as joyously as it had before.

Chapter Five

WHEN Henry Ford was six or seven years old his parents and a few neighbours noticed the boy's liking for making things. He collected every scrap of metal he could find, such as an old file, a knife blade, a clock spring, broken bits of the simple farm machinery, bolts and nuts, pieces of wood.

Even at six he was experimenting with steam from the kettle. One day he filled an earthenware jug with water, corked it tightly, and sat patiently beside it until the water generated steam. Henry wanted to learn what steam would do. He soon learned. The steam promptly obliged him by bursting the jug into a hundred fragments, scattering boiling water over the kitchen, and hurling fragments of the jug all over the place, to smash window panes and cut Henry over the head.

His startled mother bound up Henry's head and warned him against the dangers of experimenting with steam. But Henry already had learned that for himself. He had made his first important experiment, and a cut on the head seemed a small price to pay for the lesson.

All through his life, Henry experienced an impelling urge to see for himself. If an idea occurred to him, he would make something to see how that idea worked. Usually it worked about as

28

he expected it to, though occasionally he was in error. If something didn't work the first time, it might by the second or third try. If it still didn't work, he counted even that a gain: he had learned that it wouldn't work.

Failure never discouraged him. It merely suggested to him that he didn't know enough about the subject, whatever it was. And this was a habit of mind, early acquired, that he never lost. In later years, many of his ideas didn't work out as he had expected them to. He didn't care. He would carry an idea to a certain point of experiment and work, then give it up without any feeling that he had been wasting his time. He had not been wasting time; he had simply been experimenting to see what might work, and what wouldn't work with the knowledge or the means he had on hand at the moment.

Henry loved to play around the village blacksmith shop in Dearborn and to watch the blacksmith at his work. His first job in American industry probably was to pump the bellows that fed air to the forge fire. Henry was only one of many of these young volunteer firemen, who never received a halfpenny for their expenditure of energy. After school there would be anywhere from two to a dozen sturdy farm youngsters anxious to volunteer for this fascinating labour: to pump air into the forge and see the sparks fly gaily upward, to watch the iron horseshoe grow redder and redder, until it was almost white hot; then to watch the blacksmith hammer it into a desired shape and plunge it hissing into a tub of water. The blacksmith, a huge sooty magician using fire and water and iron, was as much of a hero to small boys as air-line pilots are today.

Sometimes—a special honour!—Henry would be allowed to handle the tongs and hold a horseshoe in the forge until it was hot enough to be pounded into the shape desired by the blacksmith, who could take any one of a hundred standard horseshoes and fit it to the hoof of any horse in the district. And it would fit, too, without an overlap on the hoof, although all the pounding had been done while the metal was red-hot, and with no opportunity to try it on the horse. A plunge into the water, a quick pressing of the still hot shoe against the hoof, the brief pungent smell of burning hoof to seat it firmly, and then to whip it away and plunge it again into the water for a complete cooling—that was an art that all the small boys admired, and with good reason, too, for the blacksmith is an artist in his hot and sooty realm. And if he isn't an artist he has no business near a forge or a horse.

There were many shapes into which Henry saw metal being pounded on the blacksmith's anvil. For to his shop in Dearborn came farmers from miles around with all kinds of broken farm machinery to be repaired, such as ploughs, harrows, mowing machines, rakes, shovels, scythes. The metal of which these were made was not the tough material of today; the engineering was that of the seventies, and the resulting product was somewhat less than satisfactory—except to the blacksmith, who acted as the countryside's repairman.

Then there were great iron tyres to be heated in a circular fire of coals heaped on the earthen floor, and put hot on to the wheels of wagons and quickly plunged into vats of water before they had set fire to the wooden rim of the wheel. It required nice judgment and quick handling to make everything come out just right.

In the course of a few years Henry picked up quite a store of foundry lore in the Dearborn blacksmith shop which, like others all over the country, was the forerunner of the automobile service station. In fact, although Henry never suspected it, many a country blacksmith of the seventies and eighties was to end his days in that most American of tasks—fixing Fords.

The blacksmith shop took care of his metallurgical education, but it was the old home farm that introduced Henry to carpentry and the delights of working with that most kindly and easy-going of all materials—wood. Iron and steel are tough and resistant—you have to hammer them into docility. But wood is soft and pleasant and warm to the touch; and with skill and the right tools wood will do anything you wish it to do, take any shape you ask of it, perform any task to which its strength is equal.

A farmer of the seventies was usually skilled in carpentry, and so were most of his neighbours in the villages. All repair work on buildings was done as a matter of course by the farmer and his hired hands. Only if a new barn or a house was to be built, was a professional carpenter called in. And even on those occasions the farmer and his hired men worked along with the carpenter.

Shelves, chairs, tables, cupboards were home made—and usually looked it. Axe handles, handles of ash or hickory for hoes and rakes and shovels and pitchforks were made during the slack winter season. They were cheaper than the bought ones, and usually stronger. The labour cost nothing. What did growing farm boys have hands for if not to work with? Henry learned plain carpentry and also the more intricate matter of how to make an axe handle.

He set up a little workshop for himself and there he hoarded his few tools, many of them made by himself in the Dearborn blacksmith shop. He worked happily many a winter's day, making something for the home.

He built a forge and bellows, patterned after the one in Dearborn, and naturally it worked. He had an anvil on which he could hammer hot metal into any shape he desired.

He soon began to do the repairs on broken tools and farm machinery, not only on his father's farm but on the neighbours'. By the time he was twelve he was the unofficial—and usually unpaid—repairman for the entire neighbourhood. He did it, not for profit, but because he loved the work. To repair something, to make it work again, was his chief delight. If anyone paid him, he used the money to buy more tools and materials.

Chapter Six

THE biggest event of Henry Ford's early years occurred one day when he was twelve years old. He and his father were driving along the road to Detroit when, about eight miles from the city, they encountered a road engine. It was the first vehicle not drawn by horses that Henry had ever seen, and it so impressed him that fifty years later he declared he could remember that engine as if he had seen it only yesterday.

It was a portable steam engine and boiler mounted on four wheels, with a cart hitched behind it to carry a water tank and a supply of coal. Henry had seen several of these engines being hauled around the country by horses to wherever power was needed for driving threshing machines or sawmills. But this one had a chain connection between the engine and the rear wheels of the frame on which the boiler was mounted, so the machine was moving itself.

It stopped to let the Ford farm wagon pass, and in a moment young Henry was off the wagon and talking to the driver of the road engine, a friendly man who was very proud of his mobile engine, and glad to explain it to anyone. He probably never had run across a more eager listener than young Henry Ford.

He showed him how the chain was disconnected from the

HENRY FORD

The British Ford Works at Dagenham, Essex, on the Thames

A corner of the Ford factory at Dearborn, Michigan, U.S.A.

propelling wheel and how a belt could be put on to drive a threshing machine, sawmill, or anything else in the way of machinery. He said that the engine made two hundred revolutions a minute, and that the chain pinion could be shifted to let the wagon stop while the engine kept on running. The engine had been built by Nichols, Shepard & Company of Battle Creek, Michigan, and had travelled all the way from there under its own power.

When Henry got home that night, he tried to make a model of the road engine—and, some years later, did make a model that ran very well. From that time on, he says, his great interest was in making a machine that would travel the roads—a truly amazing ambition for a boy of twelve.

The second biggest event of his twelfth year was when his father gave him a watch of his own. Shortly before that, a friend had shown him a watch that wouldn't work. Henry at once offered to find out why it wouldn't. He had no tool small enough to take a tiny screw out of a watch movement, so he made one by filing it out of a shingle nail. He found nothing wrong with that watch, but there was dust in it, so he cleaned the works and put them together again. The watch went.

When he got a watch of his own, the first thing Henry did was to take it apart to see how it worked. When he put it together again, it wouldn't go. He took it apart and studied it carefully before he reassembled it. This time it went as well as it had before he took it apart in the first place. So he promptly disassembled it again—to see if he could repeat his performance of making it go. By then he could reassemble that watch in half the time of his first operation.

That watch spent as much time disassembled as it did together, as a running timepiece. But in the course of a month, Henry knew everything about it.

Then he branched out and started on other people's watches that were out of order. Soon, in addition to his general repair business, he had a small watch and clock department in his workshop. There the non-running watches of the neighbourhood invariably would end up. If someone was seen impatiently shaking his watch, then holding it hopefully to his ear to detect a sign of movement, someone was bound to say, "Why don't

C

you take it to that Ford boy? He'll get her going." He always did, even if he had to make new parts himself.

Through his repair work he had become fairly familiar with steam engines, knew how they worked and what most frequently went wrong with them. In the neighbourhood of Dearborn there were a few of these small stationary engines, used for sawing wood and running threshing machines and for pumping water into cisterns. Henry worked on some of these and soon became more proficient at repairing them than did the Dearborn blacksmith, whose main interest was shoeing horses and putting tyres on wagons—machinery repairs were a none too well-liked side line that he worked at only because there was nobody else equipped to do it. Henry in time got most of the neighbourhood business of engine repairs, along with the blacksmith's blessing.

Early in his career as an engine repairman, Henry had a tussle with an old steam engine in an abandoned sawmill that gave him a valuable lesson on the natural animosity of inanimate objects. The cylinder head of this old engine had been removed from the cylinder, evidently to get at a valve. Whoever had removed it must have been baffled, for he had simply gone away and left it. Henry came along, stuck his arm into the cylinder to feel how the valve worked, moved something or other, and in a moment the old engine had him held fast by the arm. For an hour and a half, he says, he squirmed around among the sawdust, trying to move some part of the engine and thus release his arm. He finally succeeded. In that hour and a half he learned something about valves.

When he was thirteen, he began to build a small engine and finally constructed one that ran. And this feat, remarkable for any boy of his age, he accomplished with no materials other than pieces of scrap metal salvaged from the blacksmith shop and from broken farm machinery. That was probably Henry's first step into the automotive world: he had constructed something that ran by the power of steam.

Henry's father was not too pleased by the mechanical bent of his son. At first he was happy to have a useful mechanic about the place. It saved money for repairs. But by the time Henry was seventeen, his father was growing worried. To William Ford the finest life in the world was that of a farmer. For Henry to prefer mechanics suggested that perhaps he wasn't quite right in the head.

Henry hadn't the heart to tell his father what he really thought about farming—that it was the hardest and least rewarding labour in the world. But when he finished school he wanted to go off to Detroit and work with machinery, any kind of machinery.

"I want to go to Detroit to work, Father," he said one day, carefully choosing a time when Mr. Ford seemed to be in an especially good humour—not that he ever was an ill-humoured man.

"And what's wrong with working here, right where you are?" his father demanded.

"I want to get experience in a machine shop," said Henry. "I want to learn a lot more about machinery."

"And why should you want to be a greasy mechanic when you can be a farmer?" Mr. Ford demanded, losing some of his cheerfulness at the thought that he would be losing a pretty useful mechanic and farm hand.

"I like machines," said Henry, and let it go at that.

Mr. Ford regarded his eldest son sorrowfully and shook his head. "No good will come of it," he said. "Once a farmer, always a farmer."

Oddly enough, William Ford was right. Henry was never to lose his interest in farming, and in taking the hardest burden of farming from the back of the farmer and placing it eventually where he thought it belonged—on machinery.

"I'll be back after a while, Father," said Henry. "But I must learn more about machinery. I don't know nearly enough."

"You know enough to fix anything on the place," said Mr. Ford. "But if it's to Detroit you want to go, I'll not stand in your way."

"Thank you, Father," said Henry, who was an obedient son and very fond of his father. If his father had objected, it is quite possible that Henry would have stayed on the farm—at least for some time longer. But William Ford understood, even if he couldn't approve Henry's move. If that was what Henry wanted, to Detroit he should go, and the best of luck to him.

Chapter Seven

ONE autumn day in 1880, when Henry was seventeen, he drove with his father to Detroit. It was a very special trip for Henry Ford, for he was starting out in life entirely on his own resources, with no worldly goods other than those he carried in one trunk in the back of the wagon, along with some products of the farm.

He was a farm product himself, as much a growth of the soil as anything else in the wagon. Behind him lay seventeen years of childhood and hard work that had developed character and endurance. Perhaps, after all, he was rich—though all he seemed to own was the contents of an old trunk of his father's and five dollars in his pocket.

Detroit in 1880 was a prosperous city of a hundred thousand inhabitants, some of them the unsuspecting ancestors of men who were destined to become millionaires through their work with a vehicle then undreamed of. These ancestors already were in the ranks of industry, most of them; for Detroit was full of small machine shops and manufacturing plants, busily making things for a rapidly growing nation.

Henry Ford never for a moment questioned his chances of achieving success in the big city. He simply took it for granted that he would be successful. All he had to do was to apply himself to any task he found. And he was perfectly willing to do that—he'd been doing it for pretty much all of his life. When his father bade him good-bye and set off again for home, Henry didn't even feel lonesome. He was where he wanted to be.

The first place he went to for a job was the firm of James Flower & Co., one of the best machine shops in the city, that turned out a general line of machinery and small steam engines. The foreman took him on at once, at two-fifty a week. It never occurred to Henry that he was being exploited. That was two-fifty a week more than he had made on the farm. For his father was a thrifty man who didn't believe in paying out good money to relatives, especially his own sons, whom he naturally expected to work for him for nothing. Hadn't he worked for them all their lives, right from the cradle? Every farmer felt that way.

Henry had to look for a place to live, and was startled to find that the cheapest boarding-house that was clean and comfortable would cost him three-fifty for room and board. It didn't take Henry a moment to figure out that after working all week as an apprentice machinist and paying for his room and board, he would be a whole dollar poorer than if he had simply stayed on the farm, leaning against the side of a cow while he milked her. As Henry had arrived in Detroit with a working capital of exactly five dollars, it didn't take him more than another moment to figure that at the end of five weeks he'd be broke.

This consideration, you might think, would be enough to start a one-man back-to-the-farm movement, and thus put that Ford into reverse gear. But Henry was made of stern stuff. Besides, he wasn't fond of cows, nor did he hold any great affection for horses or pigs.

He turned up cheerfully for work next morning at seven o'clock, not only resigned to working until six that evening, but actually delighted with the prospect. He was among machinery; it was all around him in every conceivable shape and form; overhead was a canopy of moving belts to turn the machines. And he was hired as an apprentice, to learn all about it. Henry could look at machinery, feel machinery, and even smell it—a nice, warm, oily smell. Henry was happy.

He was still happy by nightfall, though he had bumped up against one slightly disconcerting fact. In theory, an apprentice in those days was there to learn—if he could find any time for learning. In practice, an apprentice found that he was expected to do everything that the machinists didn't want to do—and they quite naturally didn't want to do anything but attend to their machines and turn out pieces of metal of various shapes and sizes.

Henry found during those first days and weeks that it was the apprentice who carried chunks of metal here and there, by hand or by hand truck, who cleaned the machines, who ran errands for the mechanics, and even swept up the floors.

On that first day Henry took everything in his stride, doing all he was told to do, and also keeping in mind the fact that after a week of this backbreaking labour, and after paying his board, he would be one whole dollar poorer than if he had stayed at home. This gave him plenty to think of in idle moments during the day—he was idle sometimes for as much as five minutes before someone noticed it and said, "Here, boy—go and get me . . ." It was usually something heavy.

The moment the whistle blew and Henry and the other toilers in rugged American industry were let out, Henry went and looked for another job. Not another job in place of the one he had, but a new one, in addition. Henry had decided that in order to stay in Detroit on an apprentice's pay, he would have to work at nights, to toil while his daytime comrades rested.

He found the shop of a kindly watch repair man, a Mr. McGill, at Baker and Twentieth streets. Mr. McGill had been examining a watch through a magnifying glass screwed into one eye socket, when Henry entered the shop.

"And what can I do for you, young man?" asked Mr. McGill, taking out the magnifying glass and regarding Henry with both eyes.

"I can repair watches," said Henry. "I'd like a job."

"Rather late in the day to be looking for a job," Mr. McGill commented. "Have you just got up?"

"I've just finished work," said Henry, and briefly explained his job with the Flower Company.

"And you want to work at watch repairing instead?" Mr. McGill remarked, adding, "Well, I can hardly blame you. It's a hard life for an apprentice in a machine shop."

"Oh, it's not too hard," said Henry, "and I don't want to

work at anything instead. I want to work at watch repairing in addition, evenings.''

Mr. McGill stared at Henry in surprise. ''But you'll be too tired,'' he remarked. ''Surely, after working all day, you don't want to come here and work half the night!''

''It will be restful,'' said Henry. ''I can do it sitting down.''

''Well, for an apprentice machinist, that will be a change, anyhow,'' smiled Mr. McGill. ''When do you want to start?''

''Right now,'' said Henry. He didn't even ask what the job paid. Mr. McGill told him. It would be two dollars a week for four hours' work, six nights a week. Henry, who was good at figures, saw that this worked out to a trifle over eight cents an hour, so naturally he was delighted.

''That's fine,'' he said.

Mr. McGill told him the details. He was to start at seven sharp and work until eleven, when the shop closed. On top of his eleven hours in the machine shop, that made a working day of fifteen hours—or just about the same number of hours he had worked on his father's farm—for nothing. Now, even after paying his room and board, Henry would be a whole dollar ahead at the end of his first week, and he wouldn't have to touch a cent of his capital.

Henry started to work at once, and Mr. McGill could see that the boy knew watches. He toiled away happily until eleven that night, then went to his room and slept until six next morning, when it was time to get up and start the round all over again. All through the next day and the next, and the days that were to follow, young Henry Ford never ceased to feel thankful that he had found this first step on the road to becoming a proficient mechanic—and watch repairer.

At no time did he consider himself only a workman. The work was incidental, and he accepted it as a necessary part of life, like breathing. What he wanted to do was to acquire knowledge about mechanics: about anything mechanical. If he had to work to acquire that knowledge, it was perfectly agreeable to Henry.

That he was in any way remarkable never occurred to him. Even later in life, although he never seemed to realize it, Henry Ford was one of the most energetic individuals the world has ever produced. He was a sort of human dynamo, made to run purposefully along a single track—a production line, though the phrase had not come into use when Henry was a boy.

What Henry produced, first in his own strong, healthy young person, and later on in the persons of countless thousands of men whose efforts he directed, was simply work: movement with a single immediate purpose.

He had, from childhood, an impelling urge to make things; to take materials and turn them into something that moved, or into tools that helped to make other things. That urge guided his whole life, and is probably 90 per cent of the secret of Henry Ford's success.

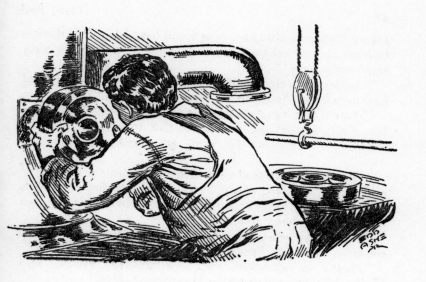

Chapter Eight

WILLIAM FORD was not a sentimental man; but he held a deep feeling of affection for his children which he seldom expressed in words. Like all fathers, he wanted his son to do well in life, so he watched with concern Henry's induction into industry—of which Mr. Ford held no high opinion.

After the boy had been working for a few months in Detroit, his father decided to have a serious talk with him. On his frequent trips to sell his farm produce he had seen the boy, briefly, had noticed that he was looking his usual self and showing no undue wear and tear due to his long hours of work. This was comforting but somewhat surprising to his father, who held the belief—generally held in those days—that work in a factory was unhealthy, leading to a gradual decline of the system. Farm work, on the other hand, was considered very healthy, despite the fact that many farmers in their later years suffered from rheumatism, backaches, and other occupational ailments attributed to years of exposure to the elements.

After inquiring how he was getting along with his work, and learning that he was happy in it, Mr. Ford remarked, "Well,

Henry, I suppose that soon now you'll have learned all there is to learn about mechanics. So then you'll be wanting to come back to the farm."

"Not for some time, Father," said Henry. "I've only started to learn a little. And there's a great deal to learn."

"There'll be a lot of work on the place this spring," remarked Mr. Ford casually, and waited for that to sink in. Then he added, "It's very healthy work on a farm—develops the muscles."

"The muscles receive considerable development in a factory," said Henry, thinking of the heavy castings he had to handle. "In fact, Father, there's too much hard labour in a factory, too much moving things around."

"Then it will be a pleasant change, no doubt, to come back to the farm," said Mr. Ford with a hopeful smile.

"There's too much hard work on a farm, too, Father," said Henry. "There's too much walking around there."

"And what's wrong with walking?" inquired his father. "It's fine exercise."

"While you're walking to a job, or taking something to the job, you're not working on the job. And there's too much of that in our factory. Why, it's like carrying water on the farm."

"And how else would you get the water from where it is in the well to where you want it?" demanded his father.

"Run it in pipes, Father, as they do here in Detroit."

"In pipes, is it!" Mr. Ford stared at his son in amazement. "And who's to pay for the pipes? Ah—and a pump, I suppose?"

"Why not?" Henry asked. "A windmill would give you enough power for that. But a steam engine would be better."

"It would be cheaper to move to Detroit, and have done with farming, once and for all," Mr. Ford commented with a trace of annoyance.

"That's just what many farm boys are doing, Father," replied Henry quietly. "They're leaving the farm and coming to Detroit to work in factories."

"The more fools they!" exclaimed Mr. Ford. "They're giving up the independent life of the farm to come to work for other men in a city."

"Father, I never felt independent on the farm," said Henry.

"The farm is the boss—not the farmer. It demands too much from him for what it gives him in return."

"A man must earn his bread by the sweat of his brow," declared Mr. Ford. "It's always been that way."

"It needn't be so for ever, Father," said Henry. "Now that we're finding more and more things to do with machines, we should be able to leave most of the hard labour to them. That would give us time to do more important things than—well, than carrying water."

"Ah, so we've come back to that city water supply system for the farm, have we?" laughed Mr. Ford. "Well, I don't hold with spending hard-earned money for citified luxuries. . . . I take it, then, you'll be staying here, son, to enjoy the turning on of a tap?"

"I'm learning what I want to learn, and that's the main thing right now, Father," said Henry. "But I don't intend to work in a factory for ever, either."

"Ah, you'll be back some day, no doubt," said Mr. Ford. "You'll find that greasy machines and noise and hurry are all very well for a time. But there's a satisfaction in watching things grow from the soil that you won't find in a city."

"I know there is, Father," said Henry. "And I'll be back one of these days, too."

"Well, no doubt we can worry along without you," said Mr. Ford, "although a hand with the harvest wouldn't come amiss."

He was a kindly man, William Ford, but he held firmly to the prevailing idea among nearly all the farmers of his day that a boy's first duty was to his parents—which, in practical terms, meant that he should stay on the farm and gradually take over more and more of the work.

Mr. Ford drove home, his day somewhat saddened by the conviction that, after all, he would have to hire an extra hand, and pay him. That seemed to him a waste of good money, to have a strong young son, working there in Detroit for a pittance —when he could be working for his own father, for nothing.

For nine months Henry toiled away happily, learning more and more about machinery and watches; how to use many and varied tools, from the tiniest watch repair tool to lathes and heavy wrenches. It was a course as comprehensive as it was peculiar, for surely no other young man in Detroit was driving himself to such divergent goals. In fact, while the newest types of engines were getting bigger, the latest styles in watches were growing smaller, the "turnip" of the seventies being supplanted by thinner varieties of timepieces.

Henry learned all he could about metalworking: how to take a piece of metal of one shape and turn it into another and more useful shape. Finally he understood how every part was made and how all these various parts were fitted together into an engine that moved—and moved to do something. That was probably the mainspring of Henry's interest in his working day: there was in the process some of the elements of original creation, elements that satisfied a craving in Henry's nature.

He read every technical journal that came his way; he studied the workings of every piece of machinery in the shop; and he did his best to understand the whole process of manufacture, so far as he could do so from his humble and restricted position—for he perforce had to spend most of his time doing hard work that was not of any benefit to him, except that it built up his muscles. Yet he accepted the work cheerfully, considering work inevitable to existence.

Henry Ford would have been the last to say so, but at the end of his nine months with the Flower Company, his was the most highly developed mind in the shop, so far as mechanics was concerned. Even though he was so new to industry, he saw much to criticize, for he was very observant.

He saw that no attempt was made to save time and labour, to bring materials to the workman, and thus keep him at his skilled work instead of forcing him to walk several miles a day to get something he needed for his job. Men wandered all over the shop, getting tools and metal. The materials never came or were brought to the men when they were needed, although casual apprentices did what they could—or what they couldn't avoid doing. The men went after this or that, stopping on the way to chat with other men, similarly wandering around. It was friendly, no doubt, but highly inefficient. And Henry, who was efficiency itself, noted it all in his receptive mind. When, years later, he had a factory of his own, nobody wandered around—

except Henry. He wandered purposefully—to see that they were on the job.

There was in that shop also, he noticed with amazement, the same moving about from task to task that he had seen on the farm. Nobody ever became a specialist at any particular job. Every workman was a mechanic who could do a hundred things, none of them particularly well. Most of them were good mechanics, but none were experts.

Nothing ever fitted. It had to be filed to the desired clearance. And there was no way to file other than by soul-chilling hand labour, back and forth, back and forth. The deadly monotony of it dismayed Henry.

It also seemed to him that the shop was trying to do too many things at once, and therefore doing none of them in the best possible way. He came to the conclusion that industry was quite as inefficient as farming. It was simply a different kind of inefficiency. He determined that he would change all that, as far as he was concerned personally. His life, he decided, would not be as cluttered up as the life of that factory.

With Henry Ford, to think was to act. Although he had received a pay increase of fifty cents a week, Henry quit his job to work for another firm for only two-fifty a week.

"I can't understand it," the foreman said, when Henry told him one day that he was through. "Here you are, leaving a job where you're doing well—and you say you're taking less at that new job?"

"I'll be learning something new," said Henry mildly. "Something worth a lot more than money."

"Nothing is worth more than money, my boy," said the foreman. "That's what it all comes to—what we're all working for, even the boss. Money!"

"I'm not," said Henry. "I don't think much of money. It's only a tool, itself. It's a means, not an end. It's like learning things; learning is a tool, too."

"Well, yes, in a way of speaking, it is," the foreman agreed. "If you learn enough, some day you might become a boss yourself, and let others do the work."

"And then what would you do with your spare time—when it was all spare time?" asked Henry.

"Just sit down somewhere," said the foreman. "That's what I'd like to do. But like enough I never will."

He wished Henry well and told him that there would always be a job waiting for him at the Flower Company if he wanted to come back. Henry thanked him, but was too tactful to say that he'd never be back. He felt that he had learned all that that job could teach him—and he was probably right. Henry was usually right throughout his life, except in a few isolated instances when he was surprisingly quite wrong.

His new employer was the Drydock Engine Company, a large manufacturing plant, twice the size of the Flower plant. It manufactured only marine engines. It was this specialization that had induced Henry to seek a job with the Drydock company; for already he had concluded that while a mechanic may do a dozen or more things fairly well, he could do only one or two things very well. He had therefore decided to put himself in a position where he could study only one thing being made— a marine engine.

Even here, he found to his surprise, the different sizes and varieties of marine engines made it impossible to specialize on only one job. Nor was there any way to avoid this; for the demand for a certain size of engine might be filled with several dozen engines, while only a few of another type could be sold. It was a limited market, and hence there could be only limited production. There was no such thing as mass production.

For two years Henry toiled away happily for the Drydock Engine Company, and in that time learned everything he could about the jobs on hand. He also read everything he could get his hands on, and kept on with his watch repair work for Mr. McGill, who didn't believe in spoiling a willing young workman by overpaying him.

At the end of three years of watch repairing, Henry was still getting only two dollars a week from the kindly, but not overgenerous old Scotchman. But Henry didn't care about money. It was interesting work, and he was learning more and more about watches, for many new watch styles were making their appearance on the market. It was the period when America was becoming time conscious, and everyone wanted a watch.

Henry gradually built up a collection of many different kinds of watches, few of which would work when he got them—which usually was the reason why they came into his possession, sometimes for a few cents, often as a gift from some customer who was buying a new watch and didn't consider the old one worth the cost of repairs. One way or another, Henry collected over three hundred watches of all makes.

During this time Henry got an idea that he didn't manage to work out to a profitable conclusion, but that undoubtedly influenced him much later on when he began building automobiles.

He had studied watches and had worked on them for so long that he came to the conclusion that all parts of a watch could be made by machinery, and made so accurately that the parts would fit without any hand labour—which was the greater part of any watch's cost.

He also had the idea that if watches could be sold in sufficient numbers to warrant a large annual production, they could be made at a cost of thirty cents. This was a revolutionary idea in the eighties, when all watches were made in small quantities with a great deal of hand labour, and with no machines in existence that would produce accurately machined parts in large numbers. The famous Ingersoll dollar watch was still in the future.

Henry set to work in his spare time to make drawings of the machines and dies for stampings, and even cut a few dies for the time when he would have a watch factory ready for production. He got a young jeweller interested in his plan, and they were on the point of trying to find the necessary capital and get their factory in operation, when Henry arrived at one of his conclusions.

"I thought that I could build a serviceable watch for around thirty cents," he says in his biography, "and nearly started in the business. But I did not because I figured out that watches were not universal necessities, and therefore people generally would not buy them. Just how I reached that surprising conclusion I am unable to state!"

By this time, Henry also had decided that he didn't like ordinary jewellery and watchmaking work, except on some new model, where the work would be interesting and hard to do.

This was at the time when standard railroad time was being arranged, when the railroads ran on standard time, and all the towns through which the trains passed still ran on sun time, with every town having time that was different, by a few minutes, from the next town. This condition presented an interesting problem to Henry, so in his spare time—working fifteen hours a day, he still had some spare time!—he succeeded in making a watch that kept both times, sun time and standard railroad time. It had two dials and was quite a curiosity in the neighbourhood of the shop. Henry also was a bit of a curiosity by now. Those who knew him marvelled at his industry.

One thing Henry gained from his abandoned plan of mass-produced watchmaking was a clear realization of the benefits of quantity machine production of a standardized article. He had figured out his costs on the basis of a production of two thousand watches a day, which he would sell wholesale for fifty cents. But then he decided that it would be impossible to sell as many as two thousand watches a day, so his plan was abandoned.

However, when he was well launched on his career of auto-mobile building, there is no doubt that his alert and retentive mind was able to utilize the thought that he had expended on the watchmaking idea. So he hadn't been wasting his time, but merely exercising his mind.

Two years with the Drydock Engine Company was enough for Henry, who in that time had managed to study every manu-facturing detail in the plant. Once he had learned that, the work no longer held any interest for him. He decided that the time had come for him to move on to new pastures. So he took a job with the Westinghouse Company as a salesman to assist one of their salesmen, John Cheeny, in selling road engines like the one he had seen when he was a boy of twelve.

This road engine was really a stationary steam engine whose power could be carried to the rear wheels of the wagon by means of a belt. Occasionally it was used as a tractor, to pull a loaded wagon, but the main purpose of its mobility was to move it by its own steam to wherever it was needed to do a job, such as running a sawmill or threshing machine. As a tractor it was inefficient; but it could creep around to its required jobs, and that was all it was designed to do.

The early Ford Assembly line at Highland Park in 1914

The final stage of assembly at Highland Park:
lowering the bodies on to the chassis

The first Ford Works in England at Trafford Park, Manchester

Young Henry was not much impressed by this smoking monster, which was very heavy and expensive. He soon learned all about it, and although he moved road engines around and serviced them for a year—chiefly during the summer months and the threshing season—his heart was not in the work. It was too routine, with nothing new to be learned. When he learned all that the road engine business had to teach him, he gave it up, as he had given up his other jobs when he had learned all that they had to teach him.

He went back to the farm for the winter, to help his father with the farm work and to carry out some experiments of his own. He now had some good shop equipment that he had bought in Detroit with every cent he could spare from his living expenses. He had a proper forge, a lathe driven by foot power, and a large collection of tools of all kinds. He also had brought back with him the ability to use these tools as an expert mechanic, and as a machinist who could make practically anything he wanted to out of metal.

"Ah, so you've come to your senses at last," said William Ford as he welcomed his son home. "I told you that you'd be back. And here you are!"

"You were right, Father," smiled Henry. "Here I am, just as you said I'd be."

It was a great satisfaction to Mr. Ford to have Henry admit that he had been right, and to ponder that now, with Henry come to his senses at last, he could dispense with the services of one farm hand, and save money. Like Henry, his father was efficient, too.

D

Chapter Nine

BACK on the farm, Henry dropped easily into the routine of farm life: getting up before daylight to milk the cows, feed the horses and pigs, and then have his breakfast before tackling the real work of the day.

Although he cared no more for farming than he had as a boy, he did his work well and cheerfully, and also found time to use his workshop, mostly on repairs to farm equipment, always in the process of wearing out. And it had worn out much faster while he was away, apparently, for it had not received the careful attention that Henry had given it.

Henry didn't miss the life in the city, for his part of that life had been the working and studying part. He had taken no time for play. While many young men who worked in the factories had relieved the monotony of their hard existence by drinking and gambling, young Henry had toiled far into the night repairing watches and studying anything he could find to read about mechanics, his eyes fixed on the future.

Henry returned to his father's farm the same quiet, well-behaved rather thoughtful young man he had been when he left. Henry never gambled, never drank, did not even smoke or chew tobacco—and in those days a young man in a factory was not considered really grown up unless he had a chew of plug tobacco distending his cheek. It was a strange habit that persisted well into the twentieth century, this chewing of tobacco.

Henry's fellow workers in Detroit had thought him an odd character. Not only was he respected but everyone liked him, even if they couldn't understand him. He made a few friends, and when he made a friend he usually kept him. Back on the farm he renewed the friendships of his boyhood, and jogged along as placidly and comfortably as he had done in the city.

The Ford home was a rather lively place, as farm homes go. Margaret Ford had grown up a very pretty girl, and the Ford home naturally became a favourite meeting-place for the young folk of the district.

During the summer they organized many picnics; and in the autumn they held a harvest supper and dance to which the young people for miles around were invited. Henry didn't dance, remarking that he could do well enough with the supper but could cheerfully dispense with the dancing, which he considered a rather aimless sort of exercise.

"You'd better learn to dance, Henry," said his sister. "Everybody dances now."

"I don't," said Henry. "I don't see any use in it."

"You'll feel rather left out of things," said Margaret, "when you see everyone dancing. Here, let me teach you a few steps. It's very easy."

"It's a waste of effort," smiled Henry. "Not that I object to dancing—but it seems so aimless, just moving around to music."

"There's more than that to it—sometimes," his sister told him with a smile. "You'll see, Henry."

Henry did see. Among the visitors was Miss Clara Bryant, a girl from Greenfield, a few miles away. She was very pretty and lively, and never had to sit out a dance. Henry had plenty of opportunity to watch her, as sitting out the dances was the only thing Henry was fitted to do. As he watched this interesting young lady gliding around in the decorous dances of the period, it suddenly occurred to Henry that he had been spending too much time with machinery, and had neglected to develop any social graces worth mentioning. He managed to exchange a few polite words with Miss Bryant, and then saw her whirled away by some young fellow who didn't know one part of a watch from another, but knew his onions, as the saying went in those days.

"Margaret," said Henry, the day after the harvest supper, "I think you're right about dancing. You do feel left out if you don't dance."

"Yes, you were left out all evening, Henry," smiled his sister. "I thought you'd see what I meant."

"I'm going to learn to dance," said Henry, and added, after a moment's thought, "If it takes all winter."

"I hear they have a dancing academy in Detroit," said Margaret. "You'll be going back soon and can start the autumn course. By Christmas, you'll be a good dancer."

"I've changed my mind about going to Detroit," said Henry. "I'll stay here—and help Father."

His father was surprised and pleased at what he thought was Henry's interest in farming. After having his fling in the big city, the boy had come to his senses and was going to be a farmer, after all.

During the next month or two, however, it seemed that Henry was taking more interest in dancing than in farming. For with his sister Margaret's help, he went at the business of learning the intricacies of dancing with the characteristic thoroughness that he had displayed in his pursuit of mechanical learning. Soon he was able to prance about with the most agile of them, taking part in every neighbourhood dance and blossoming out as a particularly lively and sociable individual, which amazed everyone who had known him since boyhood.

However, he didn't neglect his workshop, but spent many hours there building a sleigh, a slick cutter which he painted a bright crimson, visible for miles against the whiteness of the snow. In his eye-taking chariot, Henry sped about the Michigan countryside, driving to any parties where he might expect to meet Miss Clara Bryant, who for some time evinced no marked interest in his activities. He was merely one of several young men who came calling, amiable enough in his quiet way, but only another young man.

Henry, a naturally conservative youth, sought his father's

advice on the subject of matrimony. Mr. Ford pointed out that before a young man married he should have a place of his own to which to bring his bride. If Henry was serious, he'd be willing to help him get started.

Henry said that he had never been more serious in his life, so his father gave him forty acres of the old farm, part of it under cultivation, the rest bearing the original hardwood trees which he could have the pleasure of felling and sawing into lumber to build himself a house. Mr. Ford didn't believe in making things too easy for the prospective bridegroom. He pointed out that if Henry worked hard he could not only get enough lumber with which to build his house, but also could cut and sell the rest at a profit and then be able to plant crops on the cleared ground. That's the way William Ford had done, and there was no sound reason why his son should have it any easier.

Henry thanked his father for his generosity, feeling that a gift of forty acres of good Michigan farmland was indeed a generous return for all his labour. He realized then, as perhaps he had not realized before, that his father's carefulness in money matters was dictated not by selfishness but a desire to protect the interests of his family, to provide for them as they grew up.

Henry at once set to work felling the trees under which the former owners of Michigan, the Indians, had been content simply to sit. Then he rented a portable sawmill and sawed the trunks into lumber, which he left out to season. While Nature was working for him, he split some of the wood into shingles for the roof—a neat trick which only the most expert craftsman can do.

Whenever he could find the time, he would drive over to Greenfield and call on Miss Bryant, who would often go for a drive with him in his bright red cutter. However, she went for drives with other young men of the neighbourhood, too, and never missed a dance. Neither did Henry, for that matter.

Henry got his lumber seasoned during the second year of his courtship, which was about the average schedule in those days. You couldn't hurry Nature or courtships. Then he began to build his house, with the assistance of a hired man—probably Henry Ford's first employee.

He built a comfortable house, some thirty feet square, a story and a half high. If you think it's easy to build a house, just try it and see. And then recall that Henry Ford got all his lumber from his forty acres, and made it into a house himself, right from the original logs. In its way, that is as great an achievement as the gradual building of the Ford industries.

When his house was completed—and not before—Henry proposed and was accepted. In April 1888, Miss Clara Bryant and Henry Ford were married.

They didn't go to Niagara Falls on their honeymoon, as so many young couples did in those days. They didn't go any-where. They already were where they wanted to be, so Henry brought his bride to her new home on the old farm in Dearborn, just as his father had done before him.

Chapter Ten

HENRY settled down easily in double harness and went at his job of farming with enthusiasm. Wherever he could do so, he improved on existing ways of farming by using as much machinery as possible.

You would never catch Henry attached to one end of a buck-saw, bending his back up and down to cut cordwood, as nearly every farmer in the district did. With his portable sawmill, the most work Henry did was to lift the logs into position—and he even rigged up a block and tackle to handle the heavier logs. While his neighbours got tired backs, Henry stood watching the saw bite through the logs, while he figured other ways of saving himself hard work. Meanwhile, he cut and sawed timber for the neighbours, and made a rather good thing of it in the winter, when there was a minimum of work on the farm.

He developed a couple of profitable side lines so that he could employ every spare moment. He traded in cattle, and never failed to sell an animal for more than he had paid for it. He had a shrewd sense of values in cattle.

But this cattle buying and selling used up only part of Henry's time in winter. He still had some to spare, so he represented the Buckeye Harvester Company in the Dearborn district, selling and also servicing the Eclipse portable stationary engines that were used on many farms to run sawmills and pump water.

In odd moments, when he wasn't doing something immediately profitable—such as repairing watches and the farm machinery of neighbours—Henry moved his workshop from his father's farm to his own. Then he went on with his experiments with engines. He had never forgotten that first road engine he had seen trundling along the road from Detroit; and he often thought how sensible it would be to build a light mobile steam engine that would take the place of horses on the farm. More recent road engines were but little advanced from earlier models, excepting that the engine was up in front, the boiler in the rear. But they weighed over two tons and were expensive—far too expensive to be owned by any but the most prosperous farmers, with very large farms. Actually, farmers seldom bought one. They were used by people who went into the threshing business, moving from farm to farm to thresh the grain. In winter they ran sawmills. They could pull their own weight, and a threshing machine, along good roads; but they were so heavy that they bogged down in wet fields and could not be used as farm tractors at all.

Henry started to construct light steam engines and made several experimental models. To make a small one that would run well was easy enough for Henry; he was a full-fledged machinist, and could make anything. But when he made one big enough to produce the power he wanted, he found that the weight of the boiler was prohibitive.

He built a steamcar that ran very well, with a high-pressure boiler heated by kerosene. It was under the seat, and Henry decided that sitting on top of a high-pressure boiler was not altogether pleasant, if not actually dangerous. To make it heavy enough to be safe required too much weight, as he learned after two years of experimenting in his spare time. Then, although he knew that in England, where the roads were good, they had huge road engines in operation, he definitely abandoned the idea of using steam. He threw the whole idea aside, with no thought that he had been wasting his time. In fact, he had not been; for he had arrived at a sound conclusion, as the future was to show.

Henry Ford, working on his farm and experimenting with

these steam road engines, had started with the basic idea that horses were expensive and inefficient, and that the obvious thing to do was to lighten farm work by developing a tractor light enough to pull a plough or a wagon. His ambition was to take farm drudgery from flesh and blood, as he expressed it in his autobiography, and lay it on steel and motors. But as he experimented and the neighbours came around, he learned that people were more interested in something that would travel along a road and take them somewhere—a horseless carriage. Years later, he said that probably farmers wouldn't have taken to tractors if they hadn't first become used to motors in automobiles. But without waiting for the years to prove it, Henry Ford gave up the idea of a farm tractor as readily as he had given up using steam for the engine of his road car.

A few years before that, while he was working in Detroit, Henry had read in the *World of Science*, an English technical magazine, of a silent gas engine, then being built in England. It was the Otto engine, invented by a German engineer, and it ran on illuminating gas. Henry was interested in it, as he was interested in all machinery, but had concluded—rightly, as it turned out—that it was impractical. But he followed its development as well as he could, in magazine articles, and learned that the illuminating gas might be replaced by a gas formed by the vaporization of petrol. But the engine itself was heavy, with one cylinder and a large flywheel. Henry just glanced at it in passing, as it were. But he remembered it.

Then in 1885, at the Eagle Iron Works in Detroit, they installed an Otto engine. It wouldn't run, and nobody in Detroit knew anything about it. Somebody said, "That fellow Ford knows a lot about engines. Maybe he can do something with this thing." He could, and did. He not only made the reluctant Otto run, he studied it and learned all he could about it. Two years later he built an engine on the Otto four-cycle principle—by which the piston traverses the cylinder four times to get one power stroke. (This is the principle under which most modern automobile engines operate—the first, a downstroke, draws in the gas; the second, an upstroke, compresses it; the third, a downstroke, ignites it; and the fourth, an upstroke, exhausts the waste gas.)

Henry's small model worked well enough—everything Henry made worked, whether it came up to his expectations in a practical way, or not. What interested Henry was that while it was a tiny thing, with a one-inch bore and three-inch stroke, and operated with petrol, it was somewhat lighter per horsepower than the engines being offered commercially. Henry had been so bogged down by those heavy steam engines that this matter of lightness became paramount in his mind. This experiment was the real beginning of his work with the internal-combustion engine.

Henry had been making occasional trips to Detroit to sell cattle and to look over the machine shops to see if there was anything new. Henry's idea of a perfect day was to drive a herd of cattle to Detroit, sell them at a profit, and then spend a jolly afternoon walking through machine shops, learning things. To the average young man this may not appear to be a particularly stimulating way to spend a day. But Henry was not an ordinary young man; he was intent on getting ahead by means of mechanical knowledge, so walking through machine shops afforded him the keenest delight, especially when he found something new.

Years later, when he owned hundreds of miles of concrete walkways, had seen hundreds of expensive machines, all turning out parts for Fords, Henry would walk many miles a day along those pathways of industry, stopping now and then to study the operation of a particular machine, often finding that he could make its operation more efficient by making some changes.

It may have been the pleasure of being able to ramble through machine shops any day that induced Henry to return to Detroit to live. One day, when his second summer was drawing on towards autumn, he casually informed his wife that they were going to live in Detroit. Mrs. Ford was rather surprised, for she was a farmer's daughter and had never even thought of living anywhere except on a farm. But she had every confidence in Henry and his plans for building a horseless carriage. She said, "Very well, Henry," and that was that.

His father, however, was made of sterner stuff. He pointed out in no uncertain terms that his son was making a fool of himself to leave a fine farm where he had to work only fifteen hours a day to clear thirty dollars a month, cash, the year round, at the same time adding each year to the value of the farm. How could he do better than that? his father demanded.

Henry replied that he had been offered a job with the Detroit Electric Company at a salary of forty-five dollars a month. Mr. Ford shook his head sadly, and gave up arguing—even when Henry informed him that he had to go to Detroit to develop his own idea of a road car, or horseless carriage.

"This is the machine age, Father," Henry remarked. "And in the machine age horses are obsolescent, if not already obsolete. It is time the human race harnessed machinery to a wagon, and not have it dragged by horses, which are slow and inefficient. Machines are driving steamships across oceans, pulling trains of cars along rails. Why should they not propel a wagon along roads?"

"I don't hold with any such newfangled notions," said Mr. Ford. "But have your own way about it. You always do. I don't know where you get your stubborn nature. Not from me, certainly."

Henry merely smiled, and left for Detroit.

Chapter Eleven

THE horseless carriage was nothing new or revolutionary. It was well over a century old before Henry Ford even heard of it. Ninety-three years before Henry was born, a Frenchman, Nicolas Cugnot, built a three-wheeled carriage with a cumbersome steam engine turning the single front wheel. The Cugnot carriage could lumber along at between two to three miles an hour for a hundred feet or so, when it would have to stop to let the boiler build up enough steam pressure to move it another hundred feet.

In 1771 the ingenious M. Cugnot built a second machine, which still is preserved in the Conservatoire des Arts et Métiers in Paris. It also had steam trouble, being able to move only a few yards farther than its predecessor before it had to stop. M. Cugnot then called it a day, shrugged his shoulders with true Gallic resignation, and ordered a Pernod.

During the next few years many ambitious Europeans built steam-propelled cars, none of which ever generated enough steam to move them for more than a short distance, when they had to stop for breath. Some did even worse—they failed to move at all.

And yet, the hopeful inventors and builders persisted, turning out motor-car after motor-car that moved sluggishly, then stopped. These efforts caused considerable amusement to the populace, who were properly grateful for entertainment, even though they considered the inventors more than a trifle mad.

Richard Trevithick, English engineer and inventor, built a high-pressure non-condensing steam engine, which became a rival of the low-pressure steam-vacuum engine of Watt. Trevithick was a brilliant engineer and was ahead of George Stephenson in the construction of locomotive engines. On Christmas Eve, 1801, his road locomotive carried the first load of passengers ever to be conveyed by steam; and on March 24, 1802, he applied for a patent for steam engines propelling carriages.

For the next twenty years this ingenious man constructed a series of high-pressure steam engines for railroads, mines, rock-boring operations, and even to lift ballast for ships from the bottom of the Thames, at the rate of five hundred thousand tons a year, for sixpence a ton.

He built a high-pressure steam threshing engine in 1812, and told the English Board of Agriculture that he believed every process of agriculture could be performed by steam. Nearly eighty years later, Henry Ford was to conceive the same idea—and probably 99 per cent of the world's population believes that Henry was the first to think of it.

Poor Trevithick installed his steam engines in Peru and Costa Rica, then returned to England in 1827, practically penniless. The following year he petitioned Parliament for a reward for his inventions, from which England then was beginning to profit. Parliament gave him nothing. He died in poverty in 1833, his only reward his satisfaction in a great accomplishment.

There were many builders of steam-propelled road cars, starting with Evans in America in 1787; Gordon in England, 1824; James in England, 1824; another James in America, 1829; Gurney, Hancock, Church, Maceroni and Squires in England during the 1830's, and Dudgeon in America in 1857.

There was such a rash of these smoking, hissing, puffing road cars in England, and they encountered so much opposition from the wealthy stagecoach companies, that, starting in 1831, the English Parliament was induced to enact laws which within a few years practically drove steamcars from the roads. The most famous of these was the Red Flag Law, which required that a man precede the horseless carriage on foot, carrying a red flag by day and a red lantern by night. In addition, the toll roads and bridges raised their charges for the heavy steam carriages, claiming that they ruined the roads, which they probably did. The unfortunate forerunners of the automobile could no longer operate at a profit. Commercially, they passed quietly away in the middle of the nineteenth century, and did not undergo any development or make any progress in England until 1896, when the Red Flag Law was repealed.

Meanwhile in Germany and France interest turned towards the internal-combustion engine to replace the cumbersome steam power plants in their early road vehicles.

In 1885, Gottlieb Daimler, a brilliant German engineer, patented his high-speed internal-combustion engine, which soon revolutionized automotive transportation. Some ten years before this, one Siegfried Narkus, of Austria, had built a four-wheeled vehicle powered by an internal-combustion engine, but didn't patent it. Then in 1885, Benz, of Germany, produced a tricycle powered by an internal-combustion engine of his own design. A few years later, Krebs, a German, designed the first car combining many of the essential features of the modern automobile. In 1894 he designed the Panhard car in France, with a vertical engine under a hood at the front and a modern type chassis. His car also had the common type of sliding-gear transmission operated by the right hand, a clutch, and brake pedals. He even used a foot accelerator! And all of that was more than half a century ago!

By 1896 considerable work was being carried out in auto-mobile development in Germany, France, England, and the United States. The cars varied greatly in design, but they had one thing in common: as transportation they were consistently unreliable. As a wag of the period remarked in *Punch*, it took a strong-minded man to produce a car and a weak-minded one to buy it.

The motor-car is not the product of any single inventor, nor even of men within a single century. In fact, the idea goes back at least to 1686, when Sir Isaac Newton proposed a steamcar to be driven by jet propulsion—a jet of steam issuing from a nozzle in the rear of the car. Two and a half centuries were to elapse before airplane engine designers and builders of World War II produced a practical application of Sir Isaac's theories.

There were hundreds of pioneers engaged in the development of the motor-car, and only a few of them became known to fame or secured the necessary financial backing. Among European pioneers there were Daimler, Benz, Maybach, Krebs, Panhard, Levassor, Royce, Serpollet, De Dion, Bouton, Gibbon, Roots. Among prominent American pioneers were Duryea, Olds, Haynes, Winton, Ford, King, Maxwell, Apperson, Riker, Clarke, Stanley, White, and Franklin.

They produced cars in very small numbers, often having to sell their first car before they could buy material with which to build their second; and sell the second before they could start on a third, and so on, until their wives and families sometimes became slightly doubtful about them as providers. They faced many difficulties, and not among the least was the prospect of starvation.

Chapter Twelve

WHEN Henry Ford went to work for the Edison Illuminating Company of Detroit as engineer and machinist, he
moved his workshop from the farm to a shed in the rear of a
modest little house on Bagley Avenue.

He worked for the company twelve hours a day, from six in
the morning until six at night, which gave him time for experimenting and sleeping, but no time for amusements. On $45 a
month, even in those days of low prices, a man and his wife had
no money to spend on gay living, even if they had felt inclined
towards it, so Henry was fortunate that he could find interest in
his work.

It also was fortunate for him that his young wife not only
took an interest in his early experiments but believed in them
unquestioningly and felt assured that he would succeed. In appreciation of this helpful attitude, Henry called his wife The
Believer. She was almost alone in her support of his ambitions,
a fact that he never forgot and of which he spoke gratefully.

Perhaps the fact that his Dearborn neighbours, watching his
early experiments, often expressed their wonder that a man
should waste his time in such useless endeavours, had made a
great impression on Henry—though he remained as unmoved

64

The Model
'B' of 1905

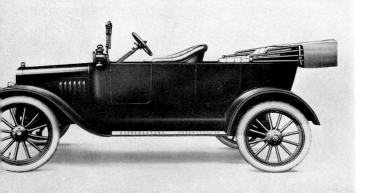

Two stages
of the
famous
Model 'T',
the 1909
and 1917
tourer
versions

1927,
the final
stage
of the
Model 'T'

In spite
of their
similarity
in appearance
there are
21 years
between
these
'Popular'
models
of 1933
and 1954

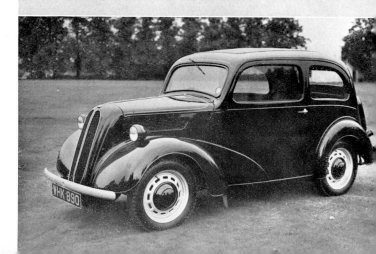

by their attitude as he was to remain towards criticism throughout his life. However, it was a great help to him that one person in the world had faith in him and didn't consider him slightly cracked. Even in Detroit, the neighbours wondered that he could work all day, and then work for half of the night.

Henry toiled away happily at the Edison plant, learning a lot about electricity and proving that he was a very useful employee. If a steam engine broke down—which it frequently did—Henry Ford could fix it. His knowledge of steam engines and his cleverness with tools impressed his employers to the extent that they soon raised his pay to $75 a month, which was tops for any mechanic in those days, even a machinist who could make parts for engines.

After only nine months, Henry was appointed chief engineer of the main plant at a salary of $100 a month, which was soon raised to $125. In a financial sense, Henry felt that he had arrived.

However, he had to work very hard, even as chief engineer. He had to be in the plant all day; and they called him back at night if anything went wrong. He had no holidays, no vacations, with or without pay. He just worked. That's what he was there for, and he did it. Oddly enough, he never considered this as anything more than a part of his schooling—a side line in life. It never seemed like hard work to him, because he was so interested in learning that the time passed quickly.

At night he would be in his little workshop behind the house in Bagley Avenue, toiling away just as happily as he had in the Edison plant. He would work by lamplight until it was time to go to bed—perhaps at dawn, if he had been engaged on something that he simply couldn't stop working on. His wife sometimes protested at this activity, urging him to rest for his own good. Henry only smiled. He wasn't tired, he'd tell her. You didn't really grow tired if you were interested enough, he'd say.

Although others were experimenting with cars, Henry Ford had no way of finding out what they were doing. Little about those early experiments was published in the newspapers or magazines. So all Henry knew was that many others were on the same track that he was on. Occasionally, he would learn of some progress in his field. But to all intents he was alone in his

E

work and had to figure everything out for himself as he went along.

His chief problems were making and breaking the spark, and trying always to cut down weight in his engine and his car, and securing suitable materials. Although he always planned each step in construction, it was a case of making something and trying it out. He could buy iron for the frame of his car, but practically everything else he made out of junk—bits and pieces of old machinery which he machined into parts. In a modern automobile factory, hundreds of parts—often including the entire body—are bought from companies that specialize in making just those things. Henry had to make every part of the first Ford car himself, including the sparking plugs—which no automobile company of today would think of making itself.

In Henry Ford's first car, the wheels were four old pneumatic-tyred bicycle wheels, and the hubs were pieces of gas pipe. The cylinders of his motor were made from the exhaust pipe of an old steam engine which Henry had bought as junk. Practically everything in the engine he had made from pieces of something else that had been junked.

He was so engrossed in his work that he was oblivious to the acid comments of his neighbours on Bagley Avenue, who were convinced that he was a crank who was trying to accomplish the impossible. Naturally, he never had any time to take his wife out for an evening, a fact upon which the neighbourhood women commented appropriately, as they will. A man who lived only to work and fool around with an invention, they declared, made a poor sort of husband. Henry heard some of these remarks at second hand, and they troubled him—but didn't stop him. Mrs. Ford was quite content with her lot, though she was sometimes annoyed when these comments were relayed to her by sympathetic friends, who hinted that perhaps the science of invention was harder on his wife than it was on the inventor. Mrs. Ford retained her belief that Henry was going somewhere. And whether he was or not, he was doing what he wanted to do, and that was all right with his kindly, devoted wife.

In 1892 the car was finished, a two-seater weighing only five hundred pounds, with the engine mounted on the rear axle. This engine had two cylinders with a half-inch bore and six-inch stroke, and developed four horse power. A small tank under the seat held three gallons of petrol that flowed by gravity to the motor through a pipe and air-mixing valve. It was ignited by a spark from a storage battery. The engine was at first air cooled, but when Henry learned that an hour's running heated it up, he put water jackets around the cylinders and piped the hot water to a tank above the engine. It was not a radiator, but in the tank the water became cooler.

The engine power was transmitted to the rear wheels by means of a belt from the motor to the countershaft, and from the countershaft to the wheels by means of a chain. The car developed two speeds, ten and twenty miles an hour, which was accomplished by shifting the belt on the countershaft by means of a clutch lever by the driver's seat. When pushed forward, the lever put the car in high speed; when pulled back, in low speed. With the lever upright, the car was out of gear—in neutral. To back the car, Henry had to get in front and push it. To stop the car, there was a foot pedal and brake.

Henry had tested the engine for many hours in his shop and was satisfied with its performance. He also had tested his transmission and brakes by moving the car a short distance in the yard. He wanted to be reasonably sure that it would work before he exposed it to the eyes of Bagley Avenue for a trial spin. Many times he discovered some defect: the engine would overheat, the petrol wouldn't vaporize properly. He would push the car back into his shop and set to work to make changes—while the neighbours smiled.

They could never look down upon him, for he had a good job and owned a farm that he had leased to a tenant. He could have been comfortable and enjoyed life, they said to one another. Yet here he was, pouring all his money and time and strength into a contraption that everybody with sense could see wouldn't get anywhere. As one farsighted individual remarked, "If God had intended man to run on wheels, he'd have put a wheel on each corner of him, instead of arms and legs." Later on, someone who may have been this gentleman's son was to remark, "If God had intended man to fly, he'd have given him wings."

One night very late, just before dawn, in April 1893, Henry

told his wife that he was at last going to give the car a trial run. It was a rainy night, the street was deserted, when Henry pushed the little car out of his shop and turned over the motor by a hand crank—thus becoming the first of countless millions who through ensuing years were to puff and pant as they started their Fords by the exercise of brute strength.

A few moments after Henry began the up-and-down-round-and-round motion that was to become a characteristic American exercise until the invention of the self-starter, the motor caught, coughed reluctantly, then settled down to work, with recurring snorts, barks, hiccups, as the mood moved it.

Henry got on to the seat and drove off, while Mrs. Ford, in a raincoat and carrying an umbrella, ran along beside him. He drove for a few blocks, turned around, and drove back triumphantly, while his startled neighbours peered from bedroom windows, amazed that at last Henry's peculiar contraption actually worked.

Henry took it all calmly. He pushed his car into the shop, drank some hot milk, and went to bed. He slept all of that day —probably the first day of his life he had spent in bed.

Henry was not satisfied with the performance of his car, and had no intention of building one to sell until he had made many changes. For weeks he drove the car about Detroit, learning many things about it that demanded improvement. Then he would put it back in the shop and go to work making new parts. The first Ford spent more time in the shop than it did in motion on the roads, where it attracted a great deal of attention, not all of it favourable.

One of man's best friends, the horse, developed an instant repugnance for the strange vehicle; and whenever it appeared, he would do his best to remove himself and whatever was attached to him from its vicinity. The sight of a horse tearing rapidly through Detroit streets with a driver hauling frantically on the reins became a not uncommon sight. Soon many horses in the city were wearing blinders, as they were called—a square piece of leather that at least cut off the horse's side view. Still, they could hear Henry's car even when they couldn't see it; and the sound of it alone was enough to terrify them. The drivers of the horses soon came to regard Henry Ford as a major nuisance, and some whose horses had run away threatened to sue him for damages.

Any vehicle that scorched through the quiet city streets at twenty miles an hour was a menace to life and limb, as a startled bicyclist proved by losing his head and running right into the car. He ended up underneath it, considerably to the surprise of Henry and himself. Passing pedestrians, who rushed to the rescue and lifted the car off him, were amazed to see him get up quite unhurt. The crowd roared with laughter, unaware that this incident was historic, probably the first automobile accident in the United States. Henry didn't see anything funny about it—it was still many years ahead of the time when the Ford joke was to become a basic part of American humour and to last until fifteen million Model T's had been run off the assembly lines.

Whenever Henry stopped and got out of his car, a crowd would gather to examine it and generally monkey with the works. If Henry left it for more than a few minutes, he usually had a minor repair job to do before he could drive off again. Once a crowd pushed it along a block, trying to get it started. Henry thereafter took no chances. He carried a chain and lock, and if he had to leave his car anywhere he locked it to a lamp-post or tree.

Henry became a problem to the Detroit police, for when he and Mrs. Ford drove anywhere a crowd collected at once, or ran along behind the car until it stopped. When this was added to the constant dashing away of frightened horses, the police bore down on Henry, threatening him with arrest as a public nuisance. He had to go to the mayor of Detroit and secure a special licence, permitting him to use the city's streets. This was the first automobile licence issued in America.

During the next three years Henry drove more than a thousand miles in the city and out into the country, trying his car on hills and finding many things that needed improvement. He was to learn that although people now were convinced that it would run, they still had no belief in the car as a method of transportation.

"Where are you going to find people with enough money to buy a thing like that?" they asked him. "And where will you find money to put up a factory and start in business?"

When he replied that he was going to make the car so cheap that almost anyone could afford to own one, they laughed and considered him as much of a crank as ever. Henry had made but little progress in the good opinion of thinking men and women, who considered that he was cracked. Just a smart mechanic who knew a lot about machinery, but nothing about human nature.

Henry kept on testing his car for three years. Then he sold it to Charley Ainsley for two hundred dollars—which he would use to buy materials for his next car, on which he began work at once. Long afterwards, he bought his first car back for one hundred dollars, and it became one of his most treasured possessions.

Chapter Thirteen

IN the same year that saw the birth of the first Ford car, Thomas A. Edison invented his motion-picture machine, and the Federal Office of Road Inquiry was established by Congressional order. Various states organized highway departments, and the movement for good roads was on. This was due largely to the bicycle craze then sweeping the country.

The bicycle-making industry in the United States was started in 1877 and reached a state of great prosperity in 1892 to 1894, by which time nearly everyone in the country had ridden on or fallen off a bicycle. It was simply the thing to do at the time, irrespective of age, sex, or physical condition. Women too frail to pedal a bicycle along the roads of those days induced their husbands to buy a "tandem" bike—a muscle-building contraption for the husband, who sat in front and pedalled for dear life, while his wife perched on the rear seat, letting her feet go idly around with the revolving pedals. Back-seat driving didn't originate with the automobile—the passenger on the lady's seat at the rear of the old tandem started the fashion, inaugurating the era of the critic in transportation.

In 1896 Henry Ford began his second car, which was much

like his first one but somewhat lighter. Tests proved it an improvement over the first model, upon which he started a third car, incorporating many new ideas and using better materials.

Meanwhile, Winton, Haynes, Duryea, and many others were building cars. They were large and so expensive that only a few rich men could afford to buy them and employ mechanics to drive and keep them in repair, for only an expert mechanic could keep the early automobile models in anything approaching regularity of operation. Even so, they were uncertain means of transportation. A man might start off happily for a ride, only to return behind a team of horses hitched to the front axle. The sardonic advice, "Get a horse!" began to be heard along the roads.

The lack of enthusiasm shown by Detroit residents was demonstrated everywhere that the early automobiles appeared. They scared the horses, and caused contented cows to look up with alarm and go running for safety to a distant corner of the pasture. They killed many a hen that was crossing the road and they constantly frightened people.

Since most of the cars' drivers were city men, this early automobiling did not tend to promote good feeling between urban and rural residents. It was claimed that passing autos so upset the cows that the milk supply was threatened, and that hens, suffering nervous breakdowns after narrow escapes from touring juggernauts, were not laying. The more pessimistic rural residents predicted a milk and egg famine, once the autos became really plentiful.

Henry Ford listened to the clamour, and kept on building his third car. In 1895 he had gone to New York to see a German Benz car on display in Macy's department store on Broadway. Henry didn't think much of the imported Benz, which was belt driven and much heavier than the Ford. Working for lightness, Henry had a poor opinion of foreign cars, all of which were heavy. This was not so much of a handicap in Europe, crisscrossed as it was by good roads. But in the United States of the nineties, with only occasional stretches of concrete paving in a few eastern states, and mud nearly everywhere, Henry Ford undoubtedly was right in his search for lightness.

Meanwhile, Henry was experiencing a little trouble with the electric company, where he was still chief engineer at a salary of $125 a month. The President of the company, as fanatically devoted to electricity as Henry was to the petrol engine, urged him to stop wasting his time with petrol. "Electricity, yes, that's the coming thing," he'd say. "But petrol—no." Henry merely smiled.

The electrically-minded president had much reason on his side, for everyone recognized that the nation was on the edge of great electrical development. Everything was going to run by electricity—at first streetcars, and finally railroad trains. What more natural than that the new horseless carriages should run by this new power?

Henry knew as much about electricity as anyone in the automobile business, and he decided that an electrical car had necessarily to be limited in its radius of operation and to contain a great weight of machinery, including heavy storage batteries, that was out of proportion to the power generated.

His opinion was confirmed by the greatest electrical wizard of his day, Thomas A. Edison, whom Henry met in 1896, when he was sent by his employer, the Edison Illuminating Company of Detroit, to attend the annual convention of the Association of Edison Illuminating Companies at Manhattan Beach, N.Y. Ford was then thirty-three, Edison forty-nine.

At dinner the main topic of conversation was the electric carriage, run by storage batteries, which many people thought was the coming thing in road transportation. It did arrive in time, flourished mildly for a few years, then drifted into the limbo of things tried and discarded, like the huge rigid dirigibles of a later period.

Somebody remarked to Edison that young Ford had built a petrol car, and pointed him out. The great inventor at once asked the man next to Ford to trade seats with him, so he could discuss the car. He asked many questions, and Henry replied to them all, even making sketches of his car and its working parts, including the insulated plug with make-and-break mechanism, forerunner of the modern plug.

Edison was enthusiastic. "Young man, that's the thing," he said. "You're on the right track, so keep on it. Electric cars must stay near power stations, and their storage batteries are too heavy. Steam cars won't do, either. They're too heavy and require a boiler and a fire. Your car is self-contained—carries its own power plant with no fire, smoke, or steam."

Here was encouragement indeed for the young car builder, who up to that moment had received no encouragement from anyone but his wife. He said later that he had hoped he was headed in the right direction, sometimes thought that he was, and sometimes only wondered if he was. But here the greatest inventive genius in the world—and the man who knew the most about electricity—had said that for a car a petrol motor was better than any electric motor could be! He returned home with renewed faith in his work.

In 1899 the electric company offered to make him general superintendent of the entire plant, provided he would give up his car and devote his energies to something useful.

"I had to choose between my job and my automobile," he said in *My Life and Work*. "I chose the automobile. Or rather I gave up the job—there was really nothing in the way of a choice. For already I knew that the car was bound to be a success. I quit my job on August 15, 1899, and went into the automobile business.

"It might be thought something of a step, for I had no personal funds. What money was left over from living was all used in experimenting. But my wife agreed that the automobile could not be given up—that we had to make or break."

It was a momentous step and a bold one to give up one of the best jobs in Detroit to enter—without any money—a business then hardly started. It had its beginnings in 1895 and only a few companies were making cars. By 1899 there were in the United States no more than 3,700 road vehicles, most of them steam propelled. There were some 500 electrics, running on storage batteries, but only 300 with petrol engines.

Conservative investors avoided the automobile business, regarding it as a wildcat speculation—as in many instances it turned out to be. But a group of Detroit men of a speculative turn of mind organized the Detroit Automobile Company to build the Ford car. Henry was made chief engineer at a salary of $100 a month. The authorized capital was $50,000, of which $10,000 was paid in. Henry was given a one-sixth stock interest in the company for the use of his car as a model.

For the next three years the little company made cars, twenty in all, on the model of the third Ford car. Henry wanted to develop better cars each year and thus find a larger market. But the backers of the enterprise had only one idea: to build cars to order, all more or less on the model of the original car. The whole thought of the group was to build no car unless they were sure of selling it, and to get the largest price possible for each custom-built car. As Henry remarked, "The main idea seemed to be to get the money."

This didn't suit Henry at all. He wasn't averse to making money; in fact, he wanted to make money. But he didn't believe that this was the way to do it. He was thinking in terms of service to the public, to build a better and always better car that would be really useful to a purchaser, instead of a headache, as most of the early cars undoubtedly were. The other stockholders couldn't see it that way, so, in March 1902, Henry Ford resigned, taking with him only his ideas and his policy. The Detroit Automobile Company later became the Cadillac Company under the ownership of the Lelands, who took it over from the original investors.

In the year that followed his resignation, Henry devoted his time to experiment and study of business conditions. In his little one-room brick shop behind his home he did a lot of work and a lot of thinking. His experience with the Detroit Automobile Company had jarred him. He wondered if business had to be such a selfish scramble for money as it seemed to be from his brief experience. From the time of his first car he had been primarily an inventor, with no immediate thought of making money until the automobile itself was much further advanced. The cars were uncertain of operation and unsatisfactory to any but a mechanic with the skill and patience to keep tinkering with them continually. They were made and sold to the public, few of whom knew how to keep them running. That didn't look honest to young Henry Ford. It didn't even look sensible. He couldn't see any sound business value in collecting more and more disgruntled customers.

During that year the automobile progressed from a machine that few people believed would run into a machine that everybody admitted would run well enough—if you knew enough

about mechanics to keep it running. The next stage of development, oddly enough, paralleled a similar stage in the development of the airplane—the primary objective was speed. As any
automobile could go faster than a horse and buggy, the public
seemed to think that the best one would be the fastest one. So,
before the automobile had got even to first base as a means of
transportation, it became a racing vehicle. Every automobile
builder felt that his cars had to show speed in races. So the
builders went into racing as a means of publicizing the automobile. If a manufacturer's special racing car won a national
race, the public would buy his other cars. If he lost, they forgot
him.

Thus the builders of cars were practically forced into the
racing game, whether or not they believed in racing. Henry
Ford was no exception. He had to attract attention to himself
and his car. As the only way of doing this was to enter the
racing game, he entered it. If racing would bring the only kind
of automobile advertising the public could be induced to read,
Henry would supply it. He would build a racing car and drive
it himself in a competition.

Chapter Fourteen

IN his big racing car, the "Bullet", Alexander Winton of Cleveland, builder of the Winton car, had become the track champion of the United States and had declared that he was ready to challenge all comers.

Henry set to work and designed a two-cylinder engine of a very compact type and fitted it into a skeleton chassis. He tried it out and it ran like the wind—in fact, it went a lot faster than the prevailing winds in the Detroit area.

He arranged a race with Winton for December 1, 1902, at the Grosse Pointe track, near Detroit. Winton was the favourite with the crowd that watched the race, for it didn't seem possible that Henry, who had never raced before, could beat the experienced Winton in his big racer. Much to the surprise of everyone except Henry, the crude-looking little Ford beat the Winton, lowering the national automobile speed record for a mile to one minute, one and one-fifth seconds. Henry now was track champion of the United States.

This impressed people more than all the cars he had built, and many offers of money to start manufacturing were made to Henry Ford. But Henry wasn't ready, for he wasn't satisfied that the automobile was sufficiently perfected yet to sell to the public. Besides, the money offered to him to start manufacturing was not on his terms: to build the best possible car for the lowest possible price—a car that anyone could operate without being a mechanical wizard.

He decided that his next step was a racing car that could beat anything in the world. Most of the new ideas concerning the automobile were being developed through racing, for the public's idea was that any first-class car should be a racer. The public was speed-conscious, and even the makers of bicycles were taking advantage of this peculiar public bias. Winning a bicycle race on a track advertised a manufacturer's other models better than anything else in the way of publicity. The automobile manufacturers were merely following a trend.

Tom Cooper, a well-known bicycle racer, joined forces with Henry in 1903 to produce two racing cars that would be known for speed and would advertise the name of Ford wherever cars were mentioned. One they named the "999", after the famous engine of the Empire State Express, the other the "Arrow". They had engines of four huge cylinders producing eighty horse power, a power at that time unheard of.

"The roar of those cylinders alone was enough to half kill a man," said Henry in his autobiography. "There was only one seat. One life to a car was enough."

Henry and Cooper tried out the cars at full speed, and Henry said that after going for a ride in them, a trip over Niagara Falls would have been a pastime. They were too much for their builders, who had no desire whatever to drive them in a race.

They decided on "999" for the first race, and still couldn't decide on a driver. Then Cooper recalled a man who lived in Salt Lake City, a professional bicycle rider named Barney Oldfield who loved speed and had told Cooper that nothing could go too fast to suit him. Cooper wired to Salt Lake City, saying that if he wanted speed, the "999" had it for him. The next train brought Barney Oldfield to Detroit. He had never driven a motor-car, but he declared that he was willing to try anything once.

It took only a week for Ford and Cooper to teach Oldfield to drive that racer. The steering wheel and gears to the front wheels had not been thought of at that time. All of Ford's cars had been equipped only with a tiller operated by one hand. On the racers Henry installed a two-handed tiller. It required all the strength of a very strong man simply to hold that car in a straight line or streaking around the curves of a race track.

The track at Grosse Pointe had curves, none of them scientifically banked, as in modern race tracks. Nobody knew how much speed any of the cars might develop, for most of them were carefully guarded before the race. Ford kept "999" as a dark horse, not even trying it out on the track. But Oldfield had learned what turns at high speed meant, and was entirely fearless. As he took his seat and Henry cranked the engine, he said cheerfully, "Well, this chariot may kill me, but they will say afterwards that I was going like hell when she took me over the bank."

And go she did, but not over the bank. Oldfield simply stared ahead and drove that car at full speed, not even shutting off power on the curves. He got around them somehow—a tribute not only to his daring but to the genius of Henry Ford, who even in his big racer had built a car that would cling to the road —because it had a low centre of gravity.

Half a dozen famous racing cars were entered in the free-for-all for the three-mile run. Oldfield took the lead at once and held it. At the finish he was half a mile ahead of the man who finished second—and some of the others were more than a mile behind him.

The *Scientific American* carried this account of the race:

> Every time Oldfield's racer started to make a turn, even though he kept close to the outside fence and turned the rear wheels very gradually, the rear end of the machine would skid around so far that the whole car appeared for a moment to be aiming straight for the inner fence. In an instant it would straighten out again, however, skim around the bend, and dart along the further side of the course at more than express train speed, only to be seen a few seconds later making its last turn amid a cloud of dust and then its final rush down the home stretch.

This marked the beginning of Barney Oldfield's career as a racing driver. He became the most famous one in the United

States. All that summer of 1903 he raced "999" and lowered his speed record several times, cutting it to 55⅘ seconds for the mile—an amazing speed on the dirt tracks of those days.

The "999" did what Henry had intended: advertised that he could build a fast car, the fastest in the country. A week after the race, he was able to form the Ford Motor Company.

Successor to the Model 'T' Ford, the 'A' of 1927

The last of the big British 'V.8's': the 'Pilot' of 1947

Chapter Fifteen

ON June 17, 1903, the Ford Motor Company was incorporated for an authorized capital of $100,000, of which only about $28,000 ever was paid in. This was the entire cash investment in the Ford Motor Company, for it never needed another dollar from an investor. The millions piled up since then have been earned solely by the company's operations.

Twelve men subscribed to the original stock issue. Henry Ford's share was 255 shares, or approximately one-fourth of the entire stock, for which he contributed his car and the right to manufacture it. He was made vice-president, designer, master mechanic and general manager of the company, with the official title of chief engineer, at a salary of $200 a month.

The company started operations in a little wooden carpenter shop on Mack Avenue, Detroit. The equipment consisted of a few models of cars and some machinery, most of it woodworking machinery. The working force was two mechanics.

As the company could not afford to buy machinery, the plan was to have various manufacturers build the parts to Ford's designs. The engines, bodies, wheels, tyres, and all parts were made by other firms, and all that the Ford company did at the start was to assemble them. Even in the way of assembling, all

the two mechanics had to do was to put on the wheels, tyres
and bodies. It was the most economical way to start building
automobiles, and the only way possible under the circumstances.

The first Ford car assembled in the little carpenter shop was
produced at the end of June and sold the first week in July.
Orders came in faster than they could be filled, and every car
was sold before it could be assembled. During the first year's
operations, the company assembled and sold 1,708 cars. The
demand was so great that the original working force of two
men was joined week by week by new men, until at the end of
the year there were forty men in the shop.

Although from the start the company was making money
there were numerous difficulties. It was often a problem to meet
pay rolls, for all the money that came in went at once into material to make more cars. But as production increased Henry found
numerous ways to cut down on the cost of manufacture and
assembly. What he cheapened was never the car itself, but the
ways of making it.

The first car produced was named the Model A. It was a two-
seater, a runabout, priced at $850, with lamps, horn, and wind-
shield extra equipment. A different body, to hold four people,
could be put on the same chassis. This touring car sold for $950.
The engine was of two cylinders delivering eight horse power.
The wheel base was seventy-two inches. The fuel tank held five
gallons.

The Ford car was lighter than any other car of its day—and it
would have been lighter if Henry had known how to make it so.
"Weight", he said, "may be desirable in a steam roller but
nowhere else. Strength has nothing to do with weight. The old
oxcart weighed a ton—and it had so much weight that it was
weak." Henry was selling transportation, not weight, and the
public soon learned of it and clamoured to buy a Ford.

The Model A was a tough, dependable car, able to stand the
hard usage of country roads. The history of one of them, the
420th car built by the Ford Motor Company, offers proof of it
indestructibility. The purchaser, Colonel D. C. Collier of California, bought it in 1904, used it two years and sold it to buy a
new Ford. The car was sold several times until 1907 when it
was bought by Edmund Jacobs who lived in the California

mountains. He drove it several years over mountain roads and trails before selling it and buying a new one. By 1915, eleven years after it had been built, it was sold to a man who took out the motor to run a water pump, and converted the chassis and wheels into a buggy. The moral, said Henry, is that you can dissect a Ford but you cannot kill it.

The early Fords were really the cars that ushered in the era of popular motoring. Until the Fords started coming out, automobiles had been made only for the rich, or at least for the fairly well to do. Cars cost all the way from $1,000 to $8,000; and those below $2,000 were very undependable, and subject to recurring breakdowns, with consequent long periods of retirement in some machine shop or blacksmith shop, waiting for repair parts. The Fords ran, and with the minimum of trouble and expense. It was a travel convenience from the start, never a luxury.

In his first advertisement, Ford said:

Our purpose is to construct and market an automobile for everyday wear and tear—business, professional, and family use; an automobile which will attain to a sufficient speed to satisfy the average person without acquiring any of those breakneck velocities which are so universally condemned; a machine which will be admired by man, woman, and child alike for its compactness, its simplicity, its safety, its all-around convenience, and—last but not least—its exceedingly reasonable price, which places it within the reach of many thousands who could not think of paying the comparatively fabulous prices asked for most machines.

The points emphasized in succeeding Ford advertising were: good material, simplicity of operation, the dependable engine, the ignition—furnished by dry cell batteries; the ease and simplicity of control, and the generally good workmanship.

Ford cars soon gained a reputation for standing up under the hardest conditions, winter and summer. Early Ford jokes featured some huge, luxurious foreign car standing on the road, with the owner crawling under it, while a Ford whizzed by. The joke, such as it was, had a solid foundation in fact. In 1903 the American public spent a million dollars for foreign cars in the high-price class, and the next year they spent two millions or more. But if any part on those cars broke, the nearest stock of spare parts was usually in New York—if it wasn't in Europe. Ford parts were in Detroit, or on the shelves of the nearest dealer—usually a machine shop owner. And the parts fitted—more or less—for precision manufacturing also was still in the future.

The automobile manufacturers followed the practice of the bicycle trade—to bring out a new model every year, so that the more prosperous owners would get rid of their old car and buy a new one. This was not Henry's idea at all. He built a car to last, and he wanted the purchaser to get the most possible use out of it. If something wore out on that car, he wished to be in a position to replace it, and at the least cost to the owner.

The plan he had in mind was to build one model of car and that every improvement on that model should be such that parts made for the new car would be interchangeable for worn-out parts on the older model. He felt that a good machine should last as long as a good watch, and that anyone who bought a Ford should not have to buy another one for a long time.

His associates, however, would not back him up in any policy so drastic. There were only so many people who could afford cars, they thought, so the thing to do was to get the wealthier ones to buy a new car each year. And to do that, of course, it was necessary to bring out new models.

In the second year, 1904, they made three models—they "scattered their energies among three models", as Henry said later. They made a four-cylinder touring car called Model B; an improved Model A, called now the Model C, and they also made Model F, a touring car at $1,000.

As they were making three models, all quite different, the manufacturing cost naturally was higher, and so was the selling price. As Henry expected, they sold fewer cars the second year than they did the first year—1,695 cars.

It became necessary to advertise the Model B, the first four-cylinder car made by Ford for general use. Although the public was beginning to think of cars as transportation, or at least as a pleasant luxury not available to all of the neighbours, racing still held the public interest. So Henry, to stimulate selling in the winter months, announced a race against time, in November, on the ice at Lake St. Claire, north of Detroit.

He took his old Arrow Racer, the twin of the more famous "999", and practically rebuilt both car and engine. A week before the New York Automobile Show, when the public became very new-car conscious, he drove it over the ice on a straight track. A large crowd assembled to watch the event, the same kind of people who attend air races or stand around an excavation watching a steam shovel at work.

It was a cold day, and the ice looked smooth enough. Certainly an automobile proceeding at a normal speed would have had no difficulty. But the ice was seamed with small cracks, and Henry knew that as soon as he attained great speed he would have trouble. If he called off the trial that day, he knew that it would result in unfavourable publicity in every newspaper in the nation. So he went ahead with the speed trial, and had the ride of his life.

The day was windy, and the straightaway course was cross wind. At every fissure in the ice, the car leaped into the air. To the onlookers it often seemed that all four wheels were off the ice—as they probably were for seconds. Henry said afterwards that he never knew how it was coming down, on four wheels or on its side. "When I wasn't in the air," he said, "I was skidding, but somehow I stayed top side up and on the course, making a record that went all over the world."

He achieved the then remarkable time of thirty-nine and a half seconds for the measured mile—cutting seven seconds off the world speed record. He also—and this had been his real purpose—won free national publicity for his Model B. But it was not enough to overcome the handicap of the price advance.

In the 1905-6 season the company made only two models—the four-cylinder car at $2,000 and a touring car for $1,000. Both of these were the previous year's models. The total sales dropped again—to 1,599 cars. This made Henry very thoughtful.

He decided that he should build only one model, and thus be in a position to sell at the lowest possible price. Most of his associates disagreed with him, so he solved the difficulty in his characteristic direct fashion. In 1906, with money he had earned and saved in the company, he bought enough stock to bring his holdings up to 51 per cent, and a little later on bought enough more to give him $58\frac{1}{2}$ per cent. His associates were glad enough to sell out at a good profit, for they were pretty sure that Henry, with his one model and low price policy, wouldn't make money in an industry that firmly believed in several models and as high a price as the traffic would bear. The Ford policy simply looked utopian to hardheaded business men.

For 1906–7, Henry stopped making touring cars and made three models of roadsters and runabouts—all of which had identical engines, chassis and parts, and differed only in the appearance of the body. The cheapest of these sold for $600 and the most expensive—the de luxe model, as we would say today—sold for only $150 more.

That year Ford sold 8,423 cars, or nearly five times as many as in any previous year. Their best week was one in May, when they assembled 311 cars in six working days. On one day in the following June they assembled 100 cars.

The year 1906 marked Ford's first investment in real estate and a building. He built a three-story plant at the corner of Piquette and Beaubien streets in Detroit. He also bought some machinery and started to make and assemble quite a number of the parts, although the car was still largely assembled from parts made by other manufacturers.

There was a demand for a large, fast car, so in 1907 Ford designed and built a big one, with a six-cylinder engine delivering fifty horse power. But although they continued turning out the small cars, the diversion to the heavy car, and the panic of 1907, cut sales down to 6,398 cars.

The Ford company, from the start, sold for cash, and directly to the individual purchaser. They gradually appointed agents in all parts of the country, setting down certain requirements and seeing that these were carried out.

Ford insisted on a suitable place of business with an adequately equipped repair shop and a stock of parts sufficient to keep every Ford car in that district in active service. He also insisted on dealer policies which insured square dealing with the customers—a radical departure from the general practice of the industry as a whole, which was to soak the customer whenever he needed a repair job. Henry's anxiety to give service along with his cars added nothing to his popularity with other manufacturers, many of whom were members of an association to control the trade. They believed that there was only a limited market for automobiles and that a monopoly of this small market was essential.

This association of manufacturers sought a monopoly under the famous Selden patent—the most amazing document ever issued by the United States Patent Office. Away back in 1879 a patent attorney named George B. Selden filed an application for a patent on, "The production of a safe, simple, and cheap road locomotive, light in weight, easy to control, possessed of sufficient power to overcome an ordinary inclination".

Mr. Selden was a lawyer, not an inventor, not even an experimenter with automobiles. But he knew patents, and the peculiar workings of the Patent Office.

He divided his claims into six groups, not one of them a new idea even in 1879, for all of them were incorporated in road engines already in existence. However, although the patent was not granted at that time, it was finally allowed in 1895, a very inclusive combination covering a carriage with its body machinery and steering wheel, with propelling mechanism, clutch and gear, and even the engine. This was all lumped into a valid patent, making Mr. Selden a very happy man.

By the time the patent was issued, many men were building automobiles. They were greatly surprised to learn that what they had made practicable was already covered by a patent granted to a man who had never had more than the idea. However, as a patent is really an invitation to a lawsuit, few of the manufacturers felt it expedient to risk an infringement and a lawsuit. So they paid Mr. Selden a royalty for every automobile they produced under the Selden licence. In a way, they felt, it was a good thing, for it kept too many people from going into the manufacture of automobiles.

In 1903 the Association of Licensed Manufacturers was formed, with ten major companies holding exclusive rights in the Selden patent. It was agreed that no firms not then in existence could join in the future, or could join only under terms agreeable to the member companies. This was the beginning of an automobile manufacturers' monopoly which would have been very harmful to the industry, for it would necessarily limit its expansion, set prices of the product, and in general work to the disadvantage of the country.

When the Ford Motor Company was organized, there were several independent manufacturers. Henry Ford had the choice of joining these independents who refused to recognize the validity of the Selden patent, or of joining the association on its own terms. After careful study, Henry decided that his car and engine were very different from cars made under the Selden patent, so he refused to recognize the validity of the patent or pay any royalty to the association.

The Electric Vehicle Company, a licensed manufacturer, brought a suit against several of the independents, including Ford. The suit dragged on from 1904 to 1909. There were thirty large volumes of testimony piled up by 1909, when Judge Hough of the United States District Court upheld the validity of the patent.

The other independents became hopeless and decided to submit to the demands of the association. Not so Henry Ford. He declared that he had just begun to fight. Nobody with a patent on a phantom car—which was about what the Selden patent actually amounted to—could tell Ford that he couldn't build a car of his own invention without paying a fee.

The association immediately replied by issuing advertisements warning prospective purchasers not to buy Ford cars. The association would sue individual owners, so everyone was warned that the moment he bought a Ford he was buying himself a lawsuit. Some wag pointed out that a lawyer should be included with the Ford tool kit, to keep the owner out of jail.

Henry snapped right back with a heavy barrage of advertising —four pages in the principal newspapers all over the nation— setting out the Ford case and saying in conclusion:

We beg to state if there are any prospective automobile buyers who are at all intimidated by the claims made by our adversaries, that we will give them, in addition to the protection of the Ford Motor Company with its some $6,000,000 of assets, an individual bond backed by a Company of more than $6,000,000 more of assets, so that each and every individual owner of a Ford car will be protected until at least $12,000,000 of assets have been wiped out by those who desire to control and monopolize this wonderful industry.

The bond is yours for the asking, so do not allow yourself to be sold inferior cars at extravagant prices because of any statement made by this "Divine" body.

N.B. This fight is being waged by the Ford Motor Company without the advice and counsel of the ablest patent attorneys of the East and West.

Henry wasn't fooling, and the country knew that he wasn't. By that time they were beginning to know the stubborn and honest character of the old farm boy from Dearborn. There was in him, they sensed, all the fighting spirit of pioneer America, not to be intimidated by the most powerful manufacturing group in the automobile industry, and not even by a United States District Court. Henry was certain that the group were wrong, and that the court was mistaken in its judgment. And he was willing to back his judgment with his entire fortune if need be. The suit eventually was decided in his favour.

The American people always root for the underdog and they rooted for Henry and his one-man war. The association had assets of $70,000,000 by 1909—and in 1903 when the battle first started, the Ford Motor Company had only $28,000. This was a natural cause for Americans to support.

And support it they did. In that year, 1909, Henry sold 18,000 cars—and no more than 50 buyers asked for indemnity bonds. If Henry was willing to fight and take a risk, so was the American public. In fact, the suit turned out to be the best of all possible advertisements. A man in a Ford felt that he was battling the evil forces of monopoly—as, indeed, he was—so he bounced happily over the roads, upheld not only by Henry's bouncy springs, but by a holy fighting spirit.

Chapter Sixteen

HENRY had started manufacturing with one basic idea: to build a simple car with the greatest strength and the least weight. From the start, he was never satisfied with the weight; he was always searching for ways in which to make the car lighter without reducing its strength.

In 1905 he was at an automobile race at Palm Beach, where a large French racing car was wrecked. After the wreck he picked up a little valve strip stem which seemed very light and strong. He asked what it was made of, but nobody knew.

Henry gave the stem to his assistant and said, "Find out all about this. That is the kind of metal we should have in our cars."

The assistant had the part analysed, and found that it was a French steel with vanadium in it. Henry then called upon every American steelmaker to find vanadium steel. None were making it; none cared to experiment. So Henry sent to England for a man who knew how to make vanadium steel commercially.

When he got his man, he found that the manufacture of vanadium requires 3,000° F., and that no ordinary American furnace could operate above 2,700°. That didn't stop Henry; it just got him nicely started.

He hunted around and found a little steel manufacturer in Canton, Ohio, who agreed to make the steel, or at least try to do it, if Henry would guarantee him against loss. Henry agreed

—and the first attempt was a failure because very little vanadium remained in the steel and therefore it wasn't much better than ordinary steel. On the second try the steel came through satisfactorily with its vanadium component. Its tensile strength was 170,000 pounds. Until then, the best American steel had a tensile strength of only 70,000 pounds.

Then Henry pulled apart his car and tested each part in detail to find out what kind of steel was best for every part. For the first time in the history of the automobile industry a manufacturer determined scientifically the exact kind and quality of steel he wanted for each part. As a result of these tests, they selected twenty different types of steel for the various parts, about ten of which were vanadium of varied kinds. The steels were selected according to whether the part was to stand hard wear or needed spring. Before that time not more than four different grades of steel had been used in the manufacture of automobiles. Further experimenting disclosed that various heat-treating methods would increase the strength of the steel—and hence reduce the weight of the car.

The vanadium steel solved one of Henry's weight problems, and simplified design solved the others. The result was that while the Ford usually looked less car than anything it passed on the roads, it was far more car for the money. And that was what Henry was after. He felt that at last he had what he called the "universal car".

In *My Life and Work* he said:

The universal car had to have these attributes: Quality in material to give service in use. Vanadium steel is the strongest, toughest, and most lasting of steels. It forms the foundation and superstructure of the cars.

Simplicity in operation, because the masses are not mechanics. Power in sufficient quantity, and absolute reliability. Lightness, control—anybody can drive a Ford. The more a car weighs, naturally the more fuel and lubricants are used in the driving; the lighter the weight, the less the expense of operation.

The less complex an article is, the easier it is to make and the cheaper it may be sold. For that reason, the greatest number may be sold to the most people. It was logical reasoning, but

among all the early automobile manufacturers, Henry Ford was
the only one to think of it. The public agreed with him and
liked the slogan he adopted, "When one of my cars breaks down,
I know I am to blame". No wonder other manufacturers began
to dislike him heartily! Whenever they had a nightmare the
central figure usually was in a Ford.

Henry had designed and built eight models in all before he
put out the famous Model T for the season 1908–9.

During that season the company also continued to produce
Models R and S, four-cylinder runabouts and roadsters, which
sold at $700 and $750. But the Model T outsold them, and it
was evident that the new models displaced the old. As Henry
says, it swept them right out. The season's sale was 10,607 cars,
a record in the industry.

Henry decided that it was time to put his policy into effect—
to sell only one model, and not to keep monkeying with styles,
trying to make the car look different each year—even if it was
actually no better.

One morning in 1910 Henry announced without any previous warning that in future they were going to build only one
model—the Model T—and that the chassis would be exactly
the same for all cars. To emphasize his point, he added: "Any
customer can have a car painted any colour that he wants so
long as it's black."

Nobody on the sales force agreed with Henry. They thought
it would be fatal to bring out this same model for next year, and
perhaps even for the year after that. They couldn't see the ad-
vantages of lowered production costs that would be the result.
When Henry said that each year the increased production would
make possible a marked lowering in the sales price, they couldn't
see that, either. They felt that lowered price would drive away
those who wanted quality, and that there would be no new
customers to replace them. They couldn't imagine that the
lower the price, the greater the number of buyers who would
come into the market. There was gloom in the sales force
especially when they read Henry's ad:

I will build a motor car for the great multitude. It will be
large enough for the family but small enough for the indivi-

dual to run and care for. It will be constructed of the best materials, by the best men to be hired, after the simplest designs that modern engineering can devise. But it will be so low in price that no man making a good salary will be unable to own one—and enjoy with his family the blessing of hours of pleasure in God's great open spaces.

His competitors liked that ad, and had a hearty laugh at it. "If Ford does that he will be out of business in six months," they said.

They told each other that a good car couldn't be built for a low price, and that even if it could be, only wealthy people bought cars anyhow—and they wanted big, expensive, impressive-looking cars. It is strange indeed that only one man in the entire industry, so far as is known, had the vision to see that Henry had a sound idea, the soundest in the industry. But then, there was only one man in the industry named Henry Ford. The rest all asked, "How soon will Henry blow up and go broke?"

While they were enjoying themselves, Henry was buying sixty acres of land at Highland Park, away out in the country west of Detroit. That was a mad move, too, they said. And so did Henry's remaining stockholders, who were perfectly satisfied with things as they had been going, and who regarded any such drastic change as a tampering with Fate. But Henry was the majority stockholder and he held control of the company's policies. There wasn't anything they could do but go along with him—and let him make them richer and richer, in spite of themselves.

Henry didn't believe in borrowing money to finance the purchase of the land and the erection of a fine factory. He thought the business should supply the money, so for the 1909–10 season he raised the prices of his cars. He sold 18,664 cars—and his competitors stopped laughing.

Then in the next season, 1910–11, by lowering his cost of production in the new factory with its greatly improved facilities, he was able to cut the cost of the touring car—and sold 34,528 cars. That was the real beginning of the steady yearly reduction in the price of cars, in spite of the ever-increasing cost of materials and the always-mounting wages.

In the years between 1908 and 1911 the factory space increased from 2·65 to 32 acres, and the average number of employees from 1,908 to 4,110. The cars built increased from 6,000 to more than 35,000.

The point that worried other manufacturers most was that while car production had increased almost six times, the working force had little more than doubled. By mass production of a single basic model, Ford had effected such economies and had so simplified production that 4,000 men could turn out as many as 10,000 cars.

During these years of development the company's business gradually had become world wide, with branches in England and Australia, where Fords were becoming well known. In 1903 two Model A's were brought to England and attracted no attention, for American bicycles had failed to stand up under use, and the impression got around that all American cars were made of bailing wire and string.

In 1905 the Ford agent entered a Model C in the Scottish Reliability Trials over 800 miles of hilly rough roads. The Ford bounced through with only one stop against it due to mechanical trouble. The resulting publicity started Fords selling in England, and in that year several were converted into taxicabs in London. The Ford won every subsequent endurance test, and sales started to mount. In 1911 a Model T was driven to the top of Ben Nevis, 4,600 feet high—and no other car had made the climb. In England 14,060 cars were sold that year, the last year in which any stunts to win publicity were attempted. An assembly plant was opened in Manchester, and eventually it became a factory making almost all parts of the car.

Chapter Seventeen

WHEN Henry Ford first announced that he would build ten thousand cars a year, the other manufacturers had laughed at him as a visionary—until 1909, when he produced more than that number. By 1916 he was producing at the rate of half a million cars a year, and on May 18, 1922 he had produced six million Model T's, by which time the daily production was five thousand cars.

Henry had apparently defied the laws of economics, as laid down by other manufacturers, and had got away with it. How had he done it?

He had studied factory methods from his early youth, and had decided that most of them were wrong: there was too much lost motion. Men wandered all over the place—getting needed tools, getting material for their work, taking pieces from here to join them to pieces over there.

In his first factory—really an assembly plant where parts manufactured by other companies were brought to be assembled into a car—the procedure was to bring every part to a certain spot as it was needed, and simply put the car together. That was

the natural, in fact the only thing to do. Then, as the company
began to make some of the parts, it was natural to set aside a
single department for this work. There one workman, or two or
more, made the parts and assembled them. But as the number of
parts increased, so did the number of workmen, until in time
they were falling over each other and getting in each other's
way. Furthermore, they had to walk farther and farther to get
needed materials and tools—just as men always had done in
factories.

Henry saw all this and came to the conclusion that the
workers were spending more time walking than they were working. It became necessary to devise ways to bring the work to the
men, rather than to have the men walking around after the work.
"Pedestrianism," said Henry, "is not a highly paid line." To
Henry it was wasted effort. So was the necessity for bending
over to pick up something.

In his mind Henry Ford formulated the basic principle that
no man should ever have to take more than one step and that
he should never have to bend over—because it tired his back and
thus decreased his efficiency. It was a simple discovery—but no
one else in factory management had thought of it.

Henry decided that the men, the tools, and the material
must be spaced in a sequence of operations that would permit
each part to travel the least possible distance from its start as
raw material to its end as a finished product.

His next step was to use slides or some form of carrier, so that
when a man completed an operation on any part he should
simply slide the part to the next man, if possible by gravity,
and if not, then by some sort of carrier such as a moving belt or
conveyor.

It was in 1913 that he tried the first experiment of an assembly line on a small part, the flywheel magneto, which one
man assembled in twenty minutes. By the time twenty-nine
men were working to assemble that part, the work was cut into
twenty-nine separate operations—one operation to a man. This
cut down the assembly time for the whole magneto flywheel to
thirteen minutes and ten seconds. A year later, Henry raised the
height of the whole line eight inches, so the men didn't have to
stoop over. And this cut the assembly time to seven minutes. As

the men could work with less physical effort, they worked faster —so the line carrying the various parts moved faster. The net result was that the assembly time was cut to five minutes—thus one man now could do as much as four men had done only a year before in the same time.

At first the motor was assembled by one man. As the number of men employed and the motors produced increased, the work was split up into eighty-four separate operations, performed by eighty-four men. The assembly time was cut to a third of what it had been.

The chassis had been assembled in one spot in an average time of twelve hours and twenty-eight minutes for each completed chassis. Henry tried the experiment of pulling the chassis down a line two hundred and fifty feet long, by means of a trolley, rope, and windlass. Six assemblers walked along beside it and picked up various parts as they went along. Much to everybody's surprise, this reduced the time to a little under six hours per chassis—or less than half of what it had been when the work stayed in one place and parts were brought to it.

Henry adopted the policy of having nobody stoop over. The work had to be at his normal standing level. However, not all men are the same height. There are tall men, short men, and medium-sized men. Henry had to compromise somewhere, so he hit upon two lines: one twenty-six and three-quarter inches and the other twenty-four and one-half inches from the floor. These heights were arrived at by long experiment and hit a fair average of the men employed when they were divided into squads suitable to their height.

The chassis now moved along waist high for most of the men —only the odd sizes having to stoop slightly or reach up at all. A further division of the work—so that each man handled only one part—cut down the assembly time per chassis to one hour and thirty-three minutes by 1914.

This may all sound simple enough, but actually it was the result of long and exhaustive study. Sometimes the line moved too fast, sometimes too slow. In the first flywheel assembly line the speed of the moving line was sixty inches per minute. That was too fast—the part was going along with men reaching to get their work done before it slid away from them. Henry put the

G

speed right down to eighteen inches per minute and gradually
increased the speed to forty-four inches per minute. That was
just right for the average workman. If he was below average in
dexterity, they transferred him to some other job where he
wouldn't have to move so fast.

They worked out speeds for each assembly, according to the
number of operations to be performed. Some men perform only
one operation, others handle several operations. One man may
place a part in position, another may fasten it. One man may put
in a bolt, the man beyond him may put on the nut—and still
another man may tighten it. And all the time the chassis, or the
engine—or whatever part it is—will be rolling along.

No part was too small to escape careful examination of means
to make it quicker, and thus cheaper. An instance is the piston
rod assembly, a very simple operation in which the workman
oiled the piston, oiled the pin, slipped the rod in place, put the
pin through the rod and piston, then tightened one screw and
loosened another one. The entire operation took three minutes,
which seemed reasonable enough until it occurred to a foreman
to analyse the motions with a stop watch. There were twenty-
eight men performing this operation, and they assembled one
hundred and seventy-five pistons and rods in a nine-hour day.
They didn't move from their bench, but had to shift along the
bench to collect the various pieces and to push away the assembled product. The foreman discovered that four hours of the
nine-hour day were actually spent moving from one part of the
bench to another—only the other five hours were spent in
assembling.

He split the operation so that one man performed only two
operations, instead of six. He installed slides so that the
finished product dropped to the next man. At once they cut
down that squad from twenty-eight to fourteen men. Later on,
when the work was further subdivided, seven men turned out
twenty-six hundred assemblies in an eight-hour day. And they
were working no harder than the original crew had been working.

This subdivision of labour has been in progress since the
start of the Ford Motor Company. By 1915 there was no more
manual handling of material. It moved on conveyer belts or by

overhead trolleys—an idea taken bodily from the meat-packing industry.

Every production line was mechanically driven, to bring the work to the men, who never moved from their appointed place along the line. Any machine that could be made automatic was made automatic—and the man who had operated it was transferred to another department or another job. Never did Henry Ford find it necessary to dismiss a workman because improved mechanical operation had made his services unnecessary. Ever-increasing production was continually opening up new jobs, lowering the price of the car, and thus widening the market for new cars.

Henry made his factory do more for him at less cost than other manufacturers of that time. The machines were placed almost side by side, with not a spare inch beyond their space requirements. To this day the Ford company believes that they put in more machinery per square foot of floor space than any other factory in the world.

There is no unused foot of floor space to increase the overhead. Yet every man has all the room he needs—but not an inch more than he needs. He may feel rather hemmed in, but he bumps into nothing. Henry, or his foremen, had decided upon the required space by scientific study, even to the detail of raising or lowering benches to fit the leg length of an individual worker so that he would be comfortable. Henry wanted everyone to be comfortable. A comfortable man works far more efficiently than an uncomfortable one—and doesn't grow so tired doing it.

Chapter Eighteen

HENRY FORD studied men as carefully as he studied raw materials, machines, and production methods: for an automobile is the net result of materials and work, which is performed by men.

His studies of factory management and of business generally had convinced him that in any large business one of the greatest problems was excess organization and excessive red tape, which usually resulted in many departments with many department heads—with impressive titles and fixed authority. If the organization was big enough, it finally got to a point where one department could communicate with another only by letters.

That never happened in the Ford company. There are no titles for executives—other than a few that are legally necessary in any company. Most men can swing a job, said Henry, but are floored by a title, which too often is used to make the title-bearer feel important and all the other working people inferior. In the Ford company the job is the important thing. The only thing that matters is the man's fitness for the job, whatever it may happen to be. There are no "positions", only jobs, and the best qualified get them.

Everybody in the Ford plants has come up from the bottom. There is not a single man anywhere in the factory who has not come off the street, through the employment department. When a man is hired nobody asks him for a testimonial as to his worthiness as a citizen. Is he willing to work? That's all there is to it.

Although everyone in the Ford plants has risen from the bottom, Henry learned that the average workman is more interested in a steady job than he is in advancement. No more than 5 per cent of those who work for wages have any desire to accept the added responsibility that goes with higher positions. Only about a quarter of the men are even willing to be foremen; and most of those who take those jobs do so only for the higher pay. The vast majority of the men simply want to stay put, to learn a job and do it with the least mental effort.

Henry said that men want to be led, to have everything done for them and to have no responsibility. In spite of the great mass of men in industry, the difficulty is not to discover men with the ability to advance, but men who are willing to be advanced.

Henry couldn't understand why this should be the case; he simply stated it as a fact, discovered through many years of experience.

Naturally, most of the jobs in a large factory are repetitive and seemingly monotonous. It has been claimed by some experts that repetitive labour is soul and body-destroying. To the more imaginative it probably would prove so. But the average man is not imaginative.

Henry cited the case of a man who all day long did nothing but step on a treadle release. This gave him lots of time to think, with the not unnatural result that he decided that he was becoming lopsided. The matter bothered him so much that he asked for a medical examination. The doctor did not find that he had been affected in any physical way, but advised a change of job. After a few weeks, the man asked for his old job back again. He missed that treadle, and was as happy as a lark when he got back to it.

A particularly monotonous task in the factory is one in which a man picks up a gear with a steel hook, shakes it in a vat of oil, then drops it into a basket. The motion never varies, and the man goes through it for eight hours a day. No muscular energy and no intelligence are required. The man does little more than wave his hands to and fro, for the gear and the little rod are light. Even Henry, who was not of a particularly sentimental nature, noticed that a certain operator had been doing this same thing for a long time, and suggested that he change to some more interesting job. The man refused. He didn't have to work hard, and he certainly didn't have to think about what he was doing. Why change jobs? He had been doing it for eight years when Henry reported the matter—and incidentally had saved and invested his wages until at that time he had $40,000. Where else could he have made $40,000 with as little expenditure of mental and physical energy?

Nobody applying for work is refused because of physical condition—except in the event of contagious disease. It was Henry's opinion that a blind man or a cripple could perform just as much work as anyone else, provided it was work that he could do. He considered that the problem was to find the jobs.

With his usual thoroughness when he got hold of an idea, Henry had every job in the plant analysed. And it turned out that there were at the time 7,882 different jobs in the factory. Of these, 949 required strong able-bodied men in perfect condition; 3,338 required men of ordinary physical development. The remaining 3,595 jobs required no physical exertion and could be performed by the weakest man, provided that he had strength enough to stand or sit down without falling over.

The lightest jobs were studied again to determine how many could be filled by legless men, one-legged men, blind men, and even armless men. It was found that 670 jobs could be filled by legless men, 2,637 by one-legged men, 2 by armless men, 715 by one-armed men, and 10 by blind men. Whenever such men turned up at the employment office, they were assigned to jobs within their powers to perform, and were paid the same wages as any other workman.

A blind man, for example, was assigned to the stock room to count bolts and nuts for shipment to branches. In two days he was able to do more than two sound men who had been doing the job, so they were transferred to other work.

Even men in the Ford Hospital were given work when they were able to sit up, and wanted something to do to occupy their minds. They were set to work screwing nuts on small bolts for the magneto department, and could do it just as well as the men in the shop. Their average was about 20 per cent above the shop average. They were paid regular wages. It was noticed that they slept and ate better and recovered more rapidly—because they were happier and occupied.

Ford discipline is strict, for in such a highly organized business confusion would be the result if every man could do as he chose. Anyone who doesn't like that system may leave.

Every machine in the Ford factories is as safe as human ingenuity can make it. Even so, a few accidents happen. When they do, the accident is analysed by a skilled man employed for that purpose, and if the machine can be further safeguarded, that is done. The machines are studied to make further accidents nearly impossible.

Ventilation is of primary concern to factory management. In all of the modern buildings the supporting columns are hollow and are made part of the ventilating system. Bad air is pumped out and fresh air is pumped in. During daylight only the sun illuminates the plant; Henry didn't believe in artificial light except for the night shift. Dark corners are painted white for cleanliness.

The reasons for accidents are: defective structures, defective machines, insufficient room, absence of safeguards, unclean conditions, bad light, bad air, unsuitable clothing, carelessness, ignorance, mental conditions of the workmen, and lack of co-operation.

"Industry," said Henry Ford, "need not exact a human toll." Where scientific study of factory management can prevent it, the Ford Motor Company prevents accidents. As a result, they have practically no serious accidents.

Henry Ford was not a sentimental person. He was not in any sense of the word paternal towards his employees. He simply believed that carelessness and inefficiency result in accidents; so he did what was humanly possibly to banish carelessness and inefficiency. That this policy has resulted in increased profits for the company is purely coincidental, a by-product.

Chapter Nineteen

HENRY FORD had never sought personal publicity. His racing he considered publicity for his cars, not for himself. By the end of 1913, although more than half a million Americans were riding in Fords, comparatively few people knew anything about him.

By the end of the first week in January 1914, his name became known to everyone in America and also over much of the world. On the evening of January 5, newspapers all over the United States carried the startling announcement that the Ford Motor Company had decided to divide with its workmen during the ensuing year a sum amounting to ten million dollars by paying a minimum wage of five dollars a day, at the same time cutting the working hours from nine to eight.

As ten million dollars was approximately half of the profits the company expected to earn that year—and half of what his stockholders expected to receive as dividends—Henry's popularity with his stockholders went down. But as the prevailing wage rate in the industry was two dollars and forty cents a day for a nine-hour day, his popularity with working men leaped skyward.

On the day after the news reached the headlines, a crowd of ten thousand men milled about the Ford plant eager to move in and start growing rich with Henry. On January 12, when the plan went into effect, twelve thousand men milled about trying to storm the factory gates. For two hours they battled with police who were vainly trying to maintain some sort of order. Very little was maintained.

The company issued a statement warning workers in nearby cities of the Middle West to stay away from Detroit. But the men came anyhow, and continued to come day after day, persuaded that the millennium had arrived. Reporters from distant cities also arrived by every train to send back to their papers frenzied accounts of the doings and to fill columns with news about Ford—who was quite as startled at the uproar he had created as were newspaper readers.

The New York *Times* expected serious disturbances to result from a policy which was "distinctly Utopian and dead against all experience".

The New York *Sun* waxed lyrical and described the Ford announcement as "a bolt out of the blue sky flashing its way across the continent and far beyond, something unheard of in the history of business". The *Evening Post* called it a magnificent act of generosity and the *World* hailed Ford as "an inspired millionaire". The Hearst papers called him "The Million Dollar Ford" and ran copyrighted illustrations of the Ford plant, the Ford farm, the first small factory, and the old racing car "999" —with Barney Oldfield at the wheel. In seven days fifty-two columns of news and views of Ford were printed in the New York papers alone. At the annual New York Flower Show a white orchid was solemnly christened "Mr. and Mrs. Henry Ford".

Henry Ford became the man of the hour, with Sunday supplement pages telling how he got his start, how Ford cars were produced, how he lived, what his hobbies were. When it turned out that his chief hobby was work, he became more of a mystery than ever. People who had never heard of Ford before were busy explaining mass production to their friends and forecasting a new era in industry when every workman would live like a king —and probably wouldn't have to work, unless he considered pushing a button or pulling a lever as work.

Naturally the net result of all the tumult was that the stock-

holders tried to stop Henry in his wild scheme to destroy profits
—just as they had tried to stop his production of a small, useful
car. Rival manufacturers declared that this time Henry really
was going broke, and predicted his early bankruptcy. Many edi-
torial writers agreed with them and proved that it was impossible to carry on a sound business with such lavish donations to
the workmen, which would only spoil them anyhow.

The president of the Pittsburgh Plate Glass Company said in
an interview, "Mr. Ford himself surely will find that he cannot
afford to pay this wage". The president of the Chalmers Automobile Company said that, "it ought to tickle the Socialists
nearly to death". But the next day a mass meeting of five hundred Socialists in Detroit denounced the raise as "an abominable
trap. By a raise of a few dollars a week Ford has purchased the
brains, life and soul of his men". But the men were still pouring
in by the trainload, eager to be "bought".

Meanwhile, Henry had been secreting himself in the less
accessible parts of his factory, trying to keep away from inquiring reporters. In the midst of the tumult he decided to slip off
to New York for a little quiet until the excitement died down.
He went to the wrong town. The moment he stepped off the
train he found reporters and photographers waiting for him at
the station. He fled to the Belmont Hotel, where, said the New
York *Herald* next morning, "Everybody in the lobby of the Belmont tried to talk at once, and the photographers were breaking down the palm trees as they endeavoured to gain a point of
vantage from which to take their pictures". Telephones to the
Ford apartment had to be disconnected and an extra squad of
house detectives was on hand. Henry stood it for three days,
then returned to Detroit.

There was no peace there, either. Reporters and photographers
continued to arrive on every train. There was no denying them
—to do so might antagonize the Press and result in unfavourable
publicity for the Ford car. Henry sighed and took it all coura-
geously. Shrewd business man that he was, he realized that this
free publicity couldn't have been purchased by the expenditure
of millions of dollars in advertising—the newspapers were advertising Fords for nothing.

Henry Ford became the most interviewed and the most photo-

graphed man in America. He posed at his desk, using his telephone to give orders; he posed walking through his plant, on the
porch of his house, at the wheel of the first Ford, at the wheel
of the latest Ford to roll off the production line. He was snapped
while shaking hands with neighbours and while patting dogs—
any stray dog that an enterprising photographer got into the
picture, for Henry owned no dog.

Henry smiled indulgently while the reporters were interview-
ing him. He had no use for Wall Street, bankers, or borrowing
money to finance a business. He was against labour unions and
butlers—he had no butler, and didn't want one. He never
smoked or drank intoxicating beverages—and didn't like to see
anyone else do it either. Alcohol he considered the fuel of the
future—not a drink. He thought farming wasteful of human
effort, believing it could be done better with machinery. He
thought railway cars too heavy—and more than twenty years
later the railroads agreed with him.

The opinions of a man whose company had made twenty million dollars in profits in the past twelve months—and that
expected to do as well or better during the next twelve—were
eagerly sought. It was taken for granted that he was bound to
know something about everything under the sun. So the reporters asked him about everything under the sun. And Henry, it
appeared, had an opinion about practically everything, including
the gold standard, free silver, tobacco, capital punishment, the
causes of war, taxation, finance, prison reform, and the theory of
evolution. As to his wage increase, he hadn't put it into effect
for business or advertising reasons, but because he regarded it as
"a plain act of social justice".

Some of his pronouncements were startling to a world that
believed he was making money by some magic formula. "The
high wage begins down in the shop," he said. "If it is not
created there it cannot get into pay envelopes. There will never
be a system invented which will do away with the necessity for
work. Nature has seen to that." This was disappointing. When
he remarked, "Work is our sanity, our self-respect, our salva-
tion", he lost a host of admirers. And when he declared that,
"So far from being a curse, work is the greatest blessing", he
was practically rambling on alone.

Before a year had passed Henry Ford was a legend, a genius
something to see—like Niagara Falls or Times Square or the
Statue of Liberty. He was an American phenomenon, and at a
mass meeting of Teddy Roosevelt's Bull Moose party in Cal-
houn County, Michigan, he was endorsed as candidate for
governor of the state.

Chapter Twenty

AFTER the first excitement had died down and the migration of eager workmen to Detroit had slowed to normal proportions, the public began to understand through numerous newspaper articles that Henry wasn't nearly as mad or as charitable as had at first been supposed. While there was no doubt that he had been moved by a sense of social justice, as he declared, there was no charity involved.

The plan was to distribute profits—not donations. And the profits had to be earned by the men themselves. But instead of waiting for the profits to be earned, the idea was to estimate them in advance and then to add them, under certain somewhat paternal conditions, to the wages of those who had been in the company's employ for six months or more.

Henry said frankly that he was building for the future, and that a business founded on low wages was always insecure. Workmen in low-wage jobs were continually growing discontented and leaving, and new ones had to be hired and trained at considerable expense. Henry had been watching men come and go for years, and he had simply decided to make it worth their while to stay—and the longer they stayed the more efficient at their jobs they would become, as a general rule.

At the beginning, the extra bonus was distributed to three classes of men: married men living with and taking good care of their families; single men over twenty-two years of age who were of proven thrifty habits; and young men under twenty-two and women who were the sole support of some next of kin. The profit rate varied according to the basic wage rate, so that a man with a low wage rate was paid a high bonus, a man with a higher wage rate, a lower bonus, so as to give each one an income of five dollars a day. And if this seems low today, it should be recalled that the average factory worker in 1914 received on the average $2.40 a day.

In 1914, when the plan was put into effect, Ford had 14,000 employees, but in order to keep that constant force of 14,000 men it had been necessary to hire 53,000 new men a year. In 1915, Ford had to hire only 6,508 new men—and most of these had been hired, not to replace those who had left, but simply because the company's business had expanded enormously. Incidentally, many of the best men in other Detroit automobile factories moved to Ford as soon as they could secure a job; so by 1915 Henry, with his plan for social justice, had the best production force procurable and the benefit of uncountable millions of dollars' worth of free publicity.

By midsummer of 1915 nearly a million Fords had come down the production line, and competitors who had been predicting that Henry would go broke were now muttering to each other that the fellow must indeed be a genius—or in league with the Devil.

Henry made changes in his bonus plan as the months and years went by, but the policy of profit-sharing through wages became a permanent Ford policy, and in good times and bad Ford paid wages as high as the conditions of the business permitted. For years the minimum was six dollars.

A month after the depression of 1929 set in for an extended stay, Ford increased his minimum rate from six to seven dollars, which remained in force until September 1931, when the previous six-dollar minimum was resumed, as the world-wide depression cut profits considerably. There was no complaint from the workers; they understood that Henry had done what he could, as he had been doing ever since 1914.

By midsummer of 1915 Ford jokes were sweeping the country. The magic of mass production seemed so incredible, with eight hundred Fords a day coming off the line, that it was inevitable that someone would remark that if a man dropped his wrench, sixteen cars with a missing bolt would scoot past him before he could pick up the wrench and do his bit.

Everybody knew a few Ford jokes, and told them to everyone he knew, until they were threadbare. Here are some: An old lady, learning that there was a shortage of tin during the war—this was the World War I—shipped a box of tin cans to the Ford factory. She received a letter from the factory service department: "Your car is in pretty bad shape, but we'll see if we can fix it up for you."

Then there was the Ford that broke down in front of a junk yard, with transmission trouble. The owner looked over the junk yard, picked out a part of an old bedspring, repaired his car and was on his way. Next day another Ford arrived minus an exhaust pipe. The owner got a section of galvanized water pipe from the junk dealer and went his way rejoicing. The dealer at once painted and hung out a sign: GENUINE FORD PARTS.

Then there was the man who hated to lose bolts and nuts that dropped off his car, so he slung a net underneath and collected them. It was also reported that a new model was coming out without doors, but equipped with a can opener—you could cut your own where you wanted them. And somebody remarked that Fords were going to be painted yellow, and sold in bunches, like bananas.

These jokes were as good publicity as any in a newspaper. You couldn't tell one without mentioning Ford. Henry enjoyed them as much as anyone, and even made up one himself, in one of his rare humorous moments.

It was his policy to buy many different makes of cars and study them. One day he was travelling from New York in a Lanchester, an expensive English automobile. A reporter along the route asked him why he was not in a Ford. "I'm on a vacation," smiled Henry. "I'm not in a hurry to get anywhere. That's why I'm not in a Ford."

Nothing lasts for ever, so the Ford joke went the way of all things and was heard no more after a year or two. But it had served one great psychological purpose: it had enshrined the bouncy little Ford in the public mind as a family friend, a standardized part of the American scene. And it had achieved what no amount of expensive advertising could do.

By the time that the Ford Joke Book could no longer be sold, even on railway trains, a million Americans were studying a new book about Fords—the Ford Manual, which told the proud owner just how to look after his Ford and get the most out of it.

Americans learned about fan belts, magneto coil springs, how to get carbon off piston heads, how to lubricate the family chariot, how to discover what was making the engine pound, or not start at all. That book, and the Ford it accompanied, really introduced the average American family to the motor age. Every owner—and his son—became a mechanic, of sorts.

There were plain diagrams in the book—every part drawn out so you could recognize it. They were numbered, so you could find each one. It was a new adventure in science just to study that book and poke around the Ford.

While Europe was going to pieces in the great war that started in August 1914, and the United States was telling itself that it could remain neutral, production in our factories boomed, prosperity increased, and on December 10, 1915, the millionth Ford car was produced.

Chapter Twenty-one

THE war that broke out in Europe in August 1914 made no single American more thoughtful than it did Henry Ford. War violated every concept of orderly, useful production for human needs on which he had based his whole life.

A life of service really was what Henry Ford had dedicated himself to with almost fanatical devotion. There is no reason whatever to doubt that the huge fortune that accrued to him was incidental to this basic conception; he was not working merely to grow richer. Henry had never cared a snap about making money, except to use it as a tool to help perform a service.

From the day he had come to Detroit to develop his car, his purpose had been to produce a useful vehicle at a low cost, and in huge numbers, for the benefit of all who could afford to own one. And after they had bought it, he wanted it to keep on serving them at the least possible expense. He wanted his cars to be used, not wasted and junked. Waste in any form was abhorrent to Henry Ford.

And war is waste, the most lavish and extravagant waste of human life and material.

Henry believed that war was a result of mismanagement, of

inefficiency in government. He probably considered a nation as a large, complex factory, and the government as the factory management. Improve the management, and all would be well, as it was in any other well-run factory.

Henry always spoke his mind freely; and as the Press was continually asking what he thought of this or that, it was only natural that they should interview him about the war and that he should say what he thought.

In many interviews, he declared that war was murderous and wasteful, that it was useless and raised a barrier to progress, and that Europe never would have stumbled into war if it had spent a thousandth part of the money on promoting peace that it had spent on preparing for war. Henry was against any nation preparing for war, even for a defensive war, and he said so in paid advertisements.

So vigorously did he proclaim his peace views that by October 1915, a number of English newspapers had refused advertisements for his car, and James Couzens had resigned as vice-president of the Ford Motor Company—because he "could not agree on Mr. Ford's public utterances on peace and preparedness". As American sympathies were generally with the Allies, Mr. Couzens's move was applauded and Henry's attitude was regarded with wonder or resentment.

Henry reacted in a way that was natural enough for him, though entirely incomprehensible to the average citizen. Here was waste and extravagance on an unprecedented scale—waste of natural resources, of costly material, of life itself—with no discernible gain for either side. The war had settled down to what was called "a war of position" by the military experts— a high-flown way of saying that both the Germans and the Allies were stuck in the mud of the trenches, with neither side making any appreciable gains. Apparently it would go on until one contender collapsed through exhaustion.

Henry's plan to end hostilities was sensible enough in theory: it was simply that, as the war had got itself into a hopeless groove, it should be ended by a negotiated peace, with the neutral nations acting as mediators in the settlement. From that would grow a proposal for the establishment of continuous mediation by a neutral agency—a League of Nations idea.

So far, Henry was firing on all four cylinders, as the more thoughtful citizens readily agreed. Nearly everybody hated war and wanted peace. And this seemed a sensible way of trying to achieve it.

At this point, Henry ran into trouble that was to result in more laughter than had ever been raised by all the Ford jokes put together. It was cruel laughter of which he was undeserving; for after all, he was only an earnest, sincere, simple and honest-minded man, trying to do something for a world in agony. And he was trying to do it in a world in which no other individual of any fame was trying to do anything whatever.

He announced that he had chartered the *Oscar II* of the Scandinavian-American line and that the ship would sail on December 4. "Some of us are going to Europe," he said and added that the company aboard the *Oscar II* were determined to do their best to bring the war to an end. "It is my earnest hope to create machinery to which those who so desire can turn to inquire what can be done to establish peace. The time has come to say, 'Cease firing'."

The war was in its second year, and not getting anywhere near an ending. Yet common sense demanded peace. Henry—and his newly found pals—would bring common sense to the scene.

There were many applicants for the free ride, including the lady who had discovered a formula for restoring health to anyone who had lost it. She figured that healthy people were naturally happy and not quarrelsome. She wanted to make everyone in Europe so happy and healthy that they'd all love each other and stop fighting. She was persistent, and the Ford officials in New York had a hard time shooing her away—especially as she was a natural for the reporters, who vied with each other in writing funny stories about the expedition.

And there was an engaged couple who wanted to be married at sea. However, the most careful screening could do little to raise the general level of sanity aboard the *Oscar II*, for most of the guests were cranks in one way or another, and all were exceedingly vocal.

It was unfortunate that the colourful pilgrimage of the peace ship completely buried the sensible idea with which Henry Ford had started: the idea of an unofficial conference between men of good will of all nations, to see what they possibly could do to help the governments of their respective nations to achieve peace. It was not a mad, or even a particularly visionary idea, unless democracy itself is a mad dream. Actually, here was democracy at work—the plain people trying to lend a hand when the official people quite obviously had got the world into a mess.

Henry had said to himself, "We plain people should do something," and he had tried to do it. That is the very basis of democracy, in the American tradition. And the people laughed at him for his pains. He never protested, but it must have hurt.

However, along at that point, something happened to Henry. His original idea was sound enough—the League of Nations that was formed after 1918, and the United Nations of today are only larger and official extensions of Henry Ford's original idea. But the concrete presence of the peace ship itself pushed into the background the sound idea of an unofficial conference of an advisory body of citizens of many nations, trying to do something that would lead to peace. Nobody heard much more about that. All they read about in the papers was the peace ship, the good old *Oscar II*, straining at its moorings, anxious to start on a practically holy crusade.

FORD CHARTERS ARK, PLANS RAID ON TRENCHES, headlined the papers. "Peace Army to sail for Europe with Auto King as Grand Commander."

That's how it went—publicity on a mass-production basis. The very mass of the peace ship publicity buried the original idea deep under big type. Even Henry forgot his idea of continuous mediation and talked of immediate action.

"We are taking out of this port a ship armed with the greatest weapon of modern times—the wireless," he declared in an interview. "We are going to use that weapon from the time we clear this port until we land in Europe. The two notes that will be sounded are faith and moral suasion." It was then that what at first had been merely a hope that a movement for peace could be started by Christmas became an active move to "get the men out of the trenches by Christmas".

Henry Ford, the real originator of mass production, had become a victim of his own assembly-line technique.

Some famous people, friends of Henry's, came aboard to wish him good luck—among them William Jennings Bryan and Thomas Alva Edison. The cheerleader shouted, "Three cheers for William Jennings Bryan," and then, "Three cheers for Thomas Alva Edison, and three cheers for Henry Ford." The passengers, all of them free riders on Henry, lustily responded. Why shouldn't they cheer for the man who was giving them a free trip to Europe, and carrying along their hobbyhorses as well?

The *Oscar II* had barely backed into midstream and turned down the Hudson when dissension broke out among the militant pacifists, each of whom had his or her own ideas about how to get the boys out of the trenches by Christmas.

Mr. Ford was ill with a bad cold and spent nearly all of his time in his cabin. By this time he must have realized the hopelessness of the undertaking, for he made no attempt to take charge of the proceedings or to influence them in any way.

Only the correspondents were happy. They reported the fights with relish, writing daily reports that resembled war communiqués. It was said that life in the trenches was peaceful compared to that aboard the *Oscar II*.

After spending six days ashore in Norway and Sweden, most of the time in his hotel suite, Henry Ford decided to return home. He left Europe on Christmas Eve, 1915—the day before the boys were to have been out of the trenches.

His quixotic adventure had failed to achieve anything but ridicule. Upon his return it was remarked that he had aged visibly, that his hair was whitening and that his smile was less frequent.

Chapter Twenty-two

Henry Ford did not lessen his efforts on behalf of peace. A neutral conference was established in Europe during 1916, with Ford paying all the bills. But naturally it could accomplish nothing, for it had no official backing by any government.

Upon his return, Henry paid for a series of peace advertisements in two hundred and fifty newspapers, attacking everything associated with war and preparedness, from warship-building programmes down to moving pictures that portrayed the defencelessness of the United States. These strange activities embroiled him in libel suits filed by the Navy League and a motion-picture company. He was learning the hard way, and making more enemies than there were Fords on the roads.

But he was making friends, too, for Americans always root for the underdog and many people sympathized with him and admired the courage that he displayed. Before the Presidential primaries of 1916, his name was placed on the Republican ballot in Michigan and Nebraska. Henry asked that his name be left off, as he sought no political office. But under the law this was impossible, as his name had been placed there by petition.

In the primary, Henry Ford carried the state of Michigan, much to the surprise of the politicians. When reporters hurried to Dearborn for an interview, "Just announce," said Henry, "that I regard this movement as a joke." He refused to be a candidate for the Republican nomination and declared that he would support President Wilson.

In 1916 the relations between Mexico and the United States were tense. On March 9, 1916, Francisco Villa with some four hundred men crossed the border, killing sixteen citizens and partly burning a town. The next day President Wilson ordered a military force into Mexico to capture Villa and his band. It had been expected that President Carranza of Mexico would co-operate with the Americans in their pursuit of Villa. Instead, he raised objections to the expedition and demanded that it be withdrawn from Mexico at once, and on June 17 notified General John J. Pershing that further invasion would be resisted by arms.

Henry Ford, with the dove of peace perched on his shoulder, was bitterly opposed to American intervention. This opposition won him a new host of enemies who attacked him in the Press with every weapon at their command, including slander and false propaganda. For instance, it was declared that he had dismissed all of his employees who were in the National Guard and had joined the Pershing expedition in pursuance of their duties. This was a deliberate falsehood, as the Ford Motor Company had kept the men's places open for them upon their return, and had aided their families during their absence in pursuit of the elusive Villa—who, incidentally, never did get caught, but lived quite happily until July 20, 1923, when some Mexican gentlemen who didn't particularly like him shot him and three companions to death.

In February 1917, the Kaiser's government announced the resumption of unrestricted submarine warfare, despite President Wilson's many protests. The President immediately recalled the American ambassador to Germany and sent the German ambassador, Count von Bernstorff, back home with a flea in his ear. He announced to Congress what he had done. There was no doubt in anyone's mind that America would enter the war.

Two days after this announcement Henry Ford went to Washington. He was a Henry so changed that his best friends and his worst enemies could hardly have recognized him. The militant pacifist had, overnight, become the embattled American.

He went at once to the Secretary of the Navy and offered the use of his plant for the construction of any war material that it could produce. He offered himself—and all his wealth and factories—to be put at the disposal of the government without profit. He offered to lend his money without a cent of interest.

"If anybody attacks the United States," said Henry, the pacifist, "believe me I am going to fight, and fight hard."

The Secretary of the Navy could not have been more surprised if he had looked out of his window and seen a rabbit biting a police dog. The only recognizable thing about this new Henry Ford was his sizing up of the industrial situation. He declared that if the war was to be won, it would be won by the nations that knew best the secrets of mass production through the standardization of one model of equipment—whatever that model should be.

Chapter Twenty-three

HENRY leaped into the war with both feet and soon the Ford factories were humming with new and unaccustomed endeavours. From April 1917 to November 1918, the Ford plants turned out tens of thousands of tons of war material, from steel helmets to steel submarine chasers and gun caissons. In addition, the plants continued to manufacture cars, trucks, and parts. They built ambulances and trucks for the Army, and even painted them khaki, instead of black, the standard Ford colour.

Henry made it clear that he wasn't in the war to make money. "I will take no profit from anything produced for any government during the war," he declared, adding, "I despise the profiteer who makes money out of war."

The Army gave Ford an order for four hundred thousand Liberty motor cylinders at twenty dollars apiece. The usual method of manufacture was to machine the cylinders from solid steel forgings. Henry decided to use steel tubing, and his engineers succeeded in devising methods and machinery, and turned out four thousand cylinders a day—at a saving of eight dollars per cylinder.

Ford built thousands of artillery caissons—and by improved manufacturing methods cut the cost five hundred dollars for each gun carriage. Henry's popularity with other manufacturers was not notably increased by these savings. It actually grieved many of them when he made two million tin hats—and cut the cost from thirty to seven cents.

Ford ran up a building a third of a mile long at the River Rouge plant and started the construction of submarine chasers —the famed Navy-designed eagle boats, which it was said rolled with such abandon that you could set a crock of cream on deck and let the boat churn it into butter. These cranky but useful craft were over two hundred feet long, and were the first ships to be built on a production line. Six months after Ford got the blueprints, the first boat slid into the Rouge River.

With his usual daring ingenuity, Ford had revolutionized shipbuilding. Keels, decks, and frames were pressed from sheet steel by machines that cut the desired pattern, punched rivet holes at the same time, and bent the metal to the right shape.

The eagle boats were two hundred and four feet long, twenty-five feet wide, drew eight feet of water. They were all steel, two thousand tons of it. They carried a crew of sixty-seven officers and men, and were armed with two four-inch and one three-inch gun, and depth bomb droppers. They were powered by oil-burning steam turbines developing three thousand horse power, built by Ford.

The first eagle boat was launched in July 1918, and had its trial trips in October. In November two more were completed. The contract was for a hundred boats, but it was changed after the armistice and sixty in all were constructed. The last one was launched in August 1919. When production was at its peak, the fastest construction time was ten days from the laying of the keel to the launching. Twenty-three were turned out in one month. If the war had lasted there is no doubt that Henry would have reached his announced objective—one ship a day. The boats cost a little over half a million dollars apiece. But if Henry had been permitted to keep going, he'd have cut that cost by a large margin.

Although Henry had changed his tactics with the war, he hadn't changed his principles. He was still a pacifist at heart and made no secret of it.

"I stand exactly where I have stood all along," he said. "But if we can't have peace without fighting for it, by all means let us fight. And let us fight in such a manner that the whole world will understand that we mean business." Nobody doubted that.

In the summer of 1918, Henry was urged to become a candidate for United States Senator, and his name was entered in both the Republican and Democratic Michigan primaries. President Wilson also asked him to run—and this was the kiss of death so far as the Republicans were concerned. If Wilson wanted Ford, the Republicans didn't.

Ford received the Democratic nomination and accepted it, but declared that he would not spend a dollar or make a speech to get himself elected. Of course, that's no way to get elected to Congress, as the Republicans soon showed him.

The Republicans nominated Truman H. Newberry, a former Secretary of the Navy, and spent a vast amount in support of their candidate—so vast that it was a violation of the federal Corrupt Practices Act, and later led to Newberry's indictment and conviction in the United States District Court.

It was a hot campaign. Leading Republicans alleged that Ford was a pacifist and that he was friendly to Germany and was hindering the conduct of the war. This was baseless slander, but anything goes in a political campaign, including an advertisement run just before the election, charging that Ford employed alleged enemy aliens in his plants. None of this was true—except that Ford was a pacifist who was willing to fight to defend his country, and to do it with no profit to himself.

Newberry was elected, and Henry retired to the depths of his factory.

He had tried to save the world with his peace plan, and had been rewarded with ridicule for his pains. Now he had tried to save Michigan from the Republicans, only to be heaped with abuse. Well, he said, that was the sort of thing one had to expect when one meddled with politics. He never meddled again.

One part of his war work gave Henry great pleasure—the farm tractor programme. All the rest of it he considered production for waste and destruction, of no benefit to humanity—other than the benefits of winning the war. But the tractor programme realized the dreams of his youth.

He had been experimenting with tractors since 1902 but did not go into the production of them until 1917, when the food emergency in Europe induced him to ship the first tractors to England, where they were operated to plough up golf courses, landed estates and other areas.

As there were not enough farm horses to take care of this extra acreage, the British government was naturally interested in power farming, and therefore conducted exhaustive tests with the small Ford tractor. It came through triumphantly, as any Ford product might be expected to do.

The British government sent Ford a cable asking him if he could produce the tractors in his Manchester plant. Henry cabled right back that he would lend his drawings of the plans, ship over as many experienced men as were needed to get the work going, and the British could produce the tractors themselves—he wanted no profit on them. However, as many of the materials could not be obtained in England, and time would be lost in setting up a factory, the government asked that five thousand tractors be made in Detroit and shipped over as soon as possible. A contract was signed, and the tractors started rolling off the lines at River Rouge, and were shipped overseas. After the war the British government congratulated the Ford Motor Company for its work, thanked Henry for his generosity, and declared that the food crisis could not have been met without the help of those tractors.

Thus England, through the war emergency, had Ford tractors for a year before they were sold in the United States. During the next ten years the handy little tractor called the Fordson made its way to farms all over the world, and helped to realize Henry's boyhood dream of lightening the drudgery of farm work.

It was used to plough and harrow, to thresh grain, run grist-mills and sawmills, provide power for pumps and other farm equipment, to pull wagons, pull stumps out of the ground, and to move buildings. On one occasion, during a coal shortage when Detroit shops were shut down, Ford used a tractor to make power for the shop that made plates for his newspaper in Dearborn.

Chapter Twenty-four

FOR America, the war had ended before the country had done more than get well started. Americans found themselves all dressed up in war emotions—and no place to go. Peacetime industries that within a few months had been converted into roaring war factories found themselves in a moment facing the prospect of reconverting their expanded war plants to peacetime work.

It was a period of chaos, materially and also psychologically—a period that came to be known as the era of postwar hysterics. Some Americans continued fighting Germany, urging a boycott of German goods. Others resurrected the Ku Klux Klan and donned nightshirts. Still others fostered "red scares"—fears of the Bolshevik threat from Russia. Everybody among the more excitable elements in the population viewed something with alarm.

National prohibition did its share to unsettle the nation. So did big business when it fought radicals who were plumping for public ownership of all public utilities. The radical called the business man a bloated capitalist, and the capitalist in turn called his opponent a Bolshevik. Certain politicians accused big business of fostering Bolshevism, while others charged the labour unions with trying to ruin the country.

Henry Ford, of all people, apparently became infected by the prevailing hysteria—a sort of national mass madness that had befuddled the wits of a considerable and very vocal percentage of the community.

Shortly after the armistice Henry had founded the Dearborn *Independent*, a modest small-town weekly which made its initial appearance without fanfare and with the expressed intention of being a conservative family-trade paper. Overnight, however, the Dearborn *Independent* blossomed out with a series of startling disclosures that was to shake the sanity of the nation and win for Henry Ford a host of new enemies and new friends.

The Dearborn *Independent* suddenly learned a surprising thing: it was "the international Jew" who was responsible for most of the troubles that plagued the world! Nobody had heard of him before that moment, but in a week he had become a reality.

The Dearborn *Independent* had learned, through a secret document, that a leadership of Jews had been established to win world domination. They were all set to sow the seeds of disruption among the Gentiles and thus eventually gain control of world finance and politics.

The disillusionment that followed the war, the higher rents, the increased costs of living, the scarcity of farm labour and the short dresses on the young women—all were blamed by the Dearborn *Independent* on that sly fellow, the international Jew— including particularly the Jews in America. It seemed they controlled the liquor business, the dress business, the cloak and suit business, and exercised an undue power over the Press by their paid advertisements.

The more susceptible and gullible among the population became alarmed, while, naturally, Jewish citizens denounced Henry and challenged him to prove any of his charges. Henry offered no proof, but the Dearborn *Independent* continued its crusade.

Resolutions were introduced into Congress; public libraries in several cities barred the Dearborn *Independent*; in Pittsburgh the police banned its sale and there were riots at local newsstands; in Toledo there was a fight in front of the Federal Building and traffic was blocked until the police could disperse the mob.

Some critics suggested that Henry had tried to borrow money from a Jewish banker and had been turned down, hence his wrath.

The Ford company replied to these charges by denying that Henry ever had tried to borrow money from any Jewish banker, that he had no animus against the Jews, and that the articles in the Dearborn *Independent* had been eminently fair, temperate, and judicial. It was simply that Mr. Ford was trying to do something about the Jewish question—thus anticipating Hitler by several years.

The Dearborn *Independent* charged along on its crusade, declaring that "statements offered in this series are never made without the fullest proof". This proof, it turned out, was contained in papers called, "The Protocols of the Learned Elders of Zion". Jewish societies all over the nation protested that these so-called Protocols were base slanders, and that there never had been an organization of Jews known as the Elders of Zion; that there never had existed a secret Jewish body organized to achieve a Jewish dictatorship.

Convinced that he had erred, Henry did what he could to make amends. "Those who know me," he said plaintively, "can bear witness that it is not in my nature to inflict insult upon and to occasion pain to anybody, and that it has been my effort to free myself from prejudice. I deem it my duty as an honourable man to make amends for the wrong done to the Jews as fellow men and brothers, by asking their forgiveness for the harm I have unintentionally committed, by retracting so far as lies within my power the offensive charges laid against their door and by giving them the unqualified assurance that henceforth they may look to me for friendship and good will."

Chapter Twenty-five

IT gradually became clear to thoughtful students of human nature that Henry Ford possessed a strange mind that ran in two sections, like the Twentieth Century Limited—if you could imagine one section of that famous train forging swiftly and safely along the water-level route between New York and Chicago, while the second section took off on its own hook and cavorted over the mountains, without benefit of tracks or noticeable control.

With his shrewd business hand at the throttle of the first section, the Ford Motor Company, Henry advanced his minimum wage to $6.00 a day—and earned a net income of $71,000,000 in the year 1919. Business boomed, and Henry Ford, as much as anyone, was to be credited with giving business confidence to progress despite the hysterical state the nation found itself in.

Through the depression of 1921, Henry declared that his confidence in America's progress was undiminished, and that even the war had brought some beneficial results through improved automatic machinery and new inventions. Things were humming so loudly on the production line that on May 15, 1921, Henry was able to tell a wondering world that Ford car No. 5,000,000 had rolled out of the greatest automobile factory in the country, at Highland Park, and that he was building one at River Rouge that would be even greater.

Henry Ford now stood alone at the helm of his gigantic enterprise, having bought out his original stockholders, one by one.

Nothing worried him as he directed the activities of 50,000 men who turned out 1,250,000 cars in the one-year period 1920–1.

At the war's end Henry brought out the Fordson in quantity production, after years of experiment in the factory and on English farms. The tractor, said Henry, was as inevitable as the motor-car, and the farmer must either take up power or go out of business.

The principle under which Ford production advanced was that Henry believed that everything could be done better—a little better or a lot better. He was ready and anxious to scrap old methods of manufacture the moment any of his engineers suggested a new and better way—usually a cheaper way.

Henry would try anything. If it succeeded, good. If it didn't, no matter. Keep on trying if you think you're on the right track, he would tell his engineers.

He had been told by metallurgists that he could not cast iron by an endless chain method. But the Ford company did it. Plate glass always had been made in a certain way—so it had to be made that way for ever, he was told. As Henry was using a sixth of all the plate glass manufactured in the United States, he thought that its cheaper manufacture was worth experimenting with. He rolled out glass on revolving drums, making it at half the price at which it ever had been made before. While experienced glassmakers were saying that it couldn't be done, Henry was doing it.

His first plan, in 1903, had been to buy manufactured parts wherever he could get them. Then, to make the parts better, he had gradually made most of the parts at the factory. But if he could have them made by other manufacturers he also let contracts. By 1921 more than 5,000 other concerns were making something for Ford. He also made the same thing in the factory, so he had a continuing check on costs. Henry never lost sight of a fraction of a cent of savings. When he found a way to do something better, and at less cost, he passed the information

I

along to his suppliers. As he went along, Henry Ford was quietly educating other manufacturers in the intricacies of mass production.

The industrial slump of 1920 caught Henry slightly off balance. In 1919 he had borrowed $70,000,000 on notes to buy the full stock interest in the Ford Motor Company. In December 1920 he still had $33,000,000 left to pay, and another $18,000,000 due or soon to become due to the government on income taxes. He had also obligated the company to pay their usual $7,000,000 bonus to the workmen. In all, he had payments totalling $58,000,000 due between January 1 and April 18, 1921—and only $20,000,000 in the bank to meet these payments.

At that time more automobile factories were closed down than were running, and most of them were in the control of banks that had loaned money to them. Even with lowered production, cars were not selling. Henry had 93,000 completed cars, and a huge stock of spare parts. But the cars weren't moving out to dealers, who couldn't get rid of the cars they already had in their salerooms.

In June of 1920, Ford sales had begun to drop. In September Henry cut prices from $575 to $440 for the touring car. That was below the cost of production, for the materials had been bought or contracted for at booming war prices. Sales increased, but soon fell off again. The public distrusted all prices now, were waiting for even lower ones.

Henry planned another cut, and kept his production at 100,000 cars a month. He knew that he would have to shut down soon, but planned to have a large stock of finished cars on hand when the shutdown came.

He wanted to open with another price cut, after which the new cars could be built from material bought at lowered prices. Henry had determined that he was paying too much for his materials. He was buying them at the rate of $50,000,000 worth a month—and Henry didn't think the stuff was worth it. The manufacturers still were hanging on to war prices—and the public was letting the finished products remain with the dealers or the manufacturers.

The Ford Motor Company shut down in December for an

announced two weeks—"to take inventory and clean house". There turned out to be so much house-cleaning to do that the plant didn't open for six weeks.

And during that time the rumours flew that Ford was in trouble. Financial editors studied the situation and agreed that it was big trouble. Henry would have to borrow, they said. There would have been no difficulty in arranging a loan. The Ford plants were worth a loan of anything up to $100,000,000.

A kindhearted banker from New York went to Detroit and called upon Henry, who was sitting at home thinking things over. He had come, like a kindly St. Bernard in the Alps, with a keg of money slung around his neck—figuratively speaking. He mentioned his genial terms—which included financial control of the company.

"But we do not wish to borrow any money," said Henry, quiet and smiling as usual.

"We know your financial condition as well as you do, Mr. Ford," said the banker. "We know that you need $75,000,000 within three months. And without our help you cannot get it."

Henry smiled and touched a bell. A servant appeared.

"Show this gentleman out," said Henry, still smiling as inscrutably as the Mona Lisa.

Henry returned to his house-cleaning. It was the biggest house-cleaning job on record. During the war the company had gone into many different kinds of war production, with dozens of new departments added. The office force had more than doubled—and now half of that force was just coasting along.

There were thirty-five Ford branches around the country, all assembling cars and many also manufacturing parts. At the time of the shutdown they stopped making parts but went on assembling cars. Henry shipped out to his branches all the parts and cars he had on hand—and said to send back the cash as soon as possible.

He telegraphed to every dealer and said that cars must be sold, that the dealers had profited in times of prosperity and that now they must help him. If they couldn't sell cars, he intimated, he'd find people who could. A Ford agency was a valuable property—not a dealer would willingly lose it. They worked like beavers, and in January 1921 they sold 60,000 cars

—when very few cars other than Fords were selling at all. By April the sales had brought in $25,000,000.

At the end of January Henry called in 10,000 men and started Highland Park into production. Junk and all machinery not actually needed in production was sold for what it would bring, irrespective of what it had cost. If it wasn't needed, it was only taking up space, said Henry. He took a good look at the office staff, cut the force in half and offered the office workers jobs in the factory. Most of them accepted the jobs.

Henry studied the forms and blanks used in production and sales—and junked half of them. He abolished every scrap of paper that didn't actually work in the production of a Ford. He had collected tons of statistics because he was interested in learning the minutest detail. He had learned that he could do without 90 per cent of them—so out they went. He got something for the waste paper.

He took out 60 per cent of the telephone extensions. He formerly had a foreman for every five men. He cut that to one foreman for every twenty men—and the former foremen went back to machines, producing cars.

He had employed 15 men per car. Now he found he could produce the car in the same time with only 9 men. The other 6 weren't fired—they just worked more efficiently. "Everything and everybody must produce or get out," said Henry.

By such means he cut the overhead charge on each car from $146 a car to $93 a car. And at a production of 4,000 cars a day, that was a saving of $212,000 a day.

Henry had faced the year with only $20,000,000 cash. On April 1 he had $87,000,000—or $27,000,000 more than he needed to meet his indebtedness. To make up this sum, he also had sold $7,900,000 worth of Liberty bonds—he had loaned his money to the country when it needed money; now he needed some himself, so he cashed in.

Financial experts who had predicted that Ford could not survive without borrowing from the banks had to recast their notions about the man who did everything differently, and did it rightly so far as his business was concerned. It was only when he climbed out of his trusty Ford and mounted one of his peculiar hobbyhorses—such as the peace ship idea or the anti-Jewish crusade of the Dearborn *Independent* that he made a joke or a nuisance of himself.

James Couzens, who knew Ford for years, said that he was the shrewdest, most far-seeing man it is possible to imagine. Now he was looking ahead to the day when he would control everything that went into the manufacture of a Ford, from coal and iron to transportation.

He bought the Detroit, Toledo & Ironton Railway, a streak of rusty rails and weatherworn, timeworn equipment consisting of 70 locomotives, 27 passengers cars and 2,800 freight cars, all in bad condition. The road ran, or crept, from Detroit south to Ironton on the Ohio River, to the West Virginia coal mines. Its 343 miles of main line and 52 miles of branches crossed several large trunk lines. Henry bought the road because its right of way interfered with plans that he had for River Rouge—and the easiest way to handle that railroad was to buy it.

Henry paid five million dollars for the road—which the experts said was more than it was worth.

He took over the road in March 1921, closed up the executive offices in Detroit—where the legal department alone had cost $18,000 a month—and put the administration in the charge of one man, who was given one-half of a flat-topped desk in the freight office from which to run the railroad.

Soon the whole track had been reballasted and miles of new rails had been laid. Locomotives and cars were overhauled at the usual Ford saving of cost. The men, better paid than they ever had been, worked with a will. The time of freight movements was cut down by two-thirds. Before Henry took over the road, it took eight or nine days to move a carload of freight to Philadelphia or New York; under Henry's prodding, that car got there in three days. Railroad men were learning from Henry how a railroad should be run. But they were against him when he wanted to cut freight rates and thus get more traffic. He made the cuts anyhow—but the Interstate Commerce Commission refused to allow them!

Henry as a railroad magnate was news—especially when it was announced that the Detroit, Toledo & Ironton was actually making money for the first time in its hopeless life. How was it possible? Henry replied that he had simply used the principles under which he ran his big Highland Park auto plant. "In our own work," he said, "we have always found that, if our principles were right, the area over which they were applied did not matter. It has never made any difference with us whether we multiplied what we were doing by five or five hundred. Size is only a matter of the multiplication table, anyway."

What Henry couldn't understand was why the big railroads, on the whole, were less successful than his little one. But he hazarded the opinion that it was because the bankers actually ran the roads as a financial proposition instead of for service. Henry never cared much for bankers.

Chapter Twenty-six

BUYING a railroad was only one step in Ford's development of what came to be known as a "vertical combination" in industry—the ownership or control of everything that went into a product, from mine and forest and transportation to the sale of the finished article.

With the Detroit, Toledo & Ironton as his mainstay, Henry could route his traffic over any one of several trunk railroads. His business was immense and eagerly sought after. What more natural, then, than for roads that wanted his business to route part of their own shipments over his now shiny rails? If Henry could get no preferential rates—because of the Interstate Commerce Commission—at least he could demand preferential treatment as to time en route for his shipments. Railroads working with Ford moved faster, as a matter of policy. Much of the speed-up in freight movements during the 1920's got its initial impetus from Henry—a fact that the railroads are loath to admit.

Henry quietly began to collect properties—a coal-field in Kentucky, timberlands in northern Michigan, coal in West Virginia. Then he built a fleet of freighters to carry his raw materials and his cars on the Great Lakes and the St. Lawrence River.

On the day when Henry celebrated his sixtieth birthday in 1923, 7,000 Ford cars rolled off the production line. More than 2,000,000 cars were made that year. In 1924 1,000,000 cars were turned out in 135 working days.

Car No. 10,000,000 came off the line on June 4, 1924, in a blaze of publicity that swept the country. The following week it left New York for San Francisco and followed the route taken by the covered wagons. Along the way it was met by reception committees and bands and led parades of old automobiles through towns along the Lincoln Highway. One of these ancient travellers was Model T No. 1,004, built in 1908, and still going strong enough to lead the parade for a few miles. Farther west a still older Ford took part, a Model F No. 482 of the Ford line, that had made its first journey west in 1905.

If Henry Ford had driven that ten millionth Ford himself and had made speeches in the cities the car passed through, it is quite possible that he could have become President of the United States.

The "Ford for President" boom that swept the country in 1923 had its start in Dearborn a few months before, when a hundred or more of Henry's neighbours held a meeting, made speeches, and came out with the slogan, "We want Henry". Henry paid no attention, made no contribution to any of the three hundred Ford for President clubs that shortly were organized in many sections of the country. He had meant it when, at the end of his Senatorial campaigns—in which he did no campaigning—he had declared that he was through with politics.

But the Ford for President boom grew, and by the summer of 1923 it had assumed proportions that amazed politicians. Senator King of Utah declared at the time that if elections were held at that moment, Ford would sweep the country; and the newspapers reported that the growth of popular sentiment for Ford was causing deep anxiety and concern to both Republicans and Democrats. Ford had said on an earlier occasion that he didn't see much difference in those parties and that "they both are tarred by the same brush". That was no way to win the support of a Republican or a Democratic politician.

But the voters liked Henry, despite his unorthodox opinions on various matters. They figured that if he had brains enough to build the greatest industry in the world, with assets larger than those of United States Steel, he also might be smart enough to run the United States. The United States was a business that should be run along business lines. Who was a shrewder business man than Henry?

A *Collier's* poll showed Ford leading the President eight to five and his nearest rival five to one, and carrying every state west of the Mississippi, and every state east of the Mississippi except three in New England. The New York *Herald Tribune* thought that "Ford would run like wildfire in the western country".

Statements were issued by senators from the West predicting that Ford would be nominated if the party leaders followed the wishes of the people—one of the last things party leaders care to follow. Will Rogers surmised that Ford was as good as elected if he would promise the nation a new hood for the Ford car.

The boom collapsed for one reason, and one reason only. Henry refused to take any part in it, insisting that he was not in politics, not interested, not a candidate. Even the most enthusiastic jockey can't make his horse win a race if the horse doesn't choose to run. No amount of pleading could move Henry. He had been cured of politics.

But if Henry had only agreed to run! And if he had stumped the country in that ten millionth Ford! With Henry Ford as President, American history during ensuing years might have been vastly different. This much seems certain: the cost of government would have been lowered appreciably, and the efficiency of government bureaux would have been increased. Henry was an expert on house-cleaning, and it would be only natural for him to apply his rule that "everything and everybody must produce or get out". Perhaps that is what the politicians were really afraid of.

Henry attended to his knitting—knitting together the threads of the greatest industrial fabric ever woven by one man. Although the brain and the brawn of tens of thousands of executives and workmen went into the process, it still was true that all of this vast empire was but the lengthened shadow of Henry Ford. As great as that empire was, Henry towered above it in the public mind. His successes overshadowed his failures; his understanding, his helpfulness, his honest desire to do what he could to make life better and more secure for the workers in his factories, made the average citizen forget or forgive his errors. After all, when a man can pile up a fortune of a billion dollars —and not make anybody poorer in the process—he must have been more right than wrong, for most of the time. "We like old Henry", was the general verdict. But there is no evidence that Henry ever cared whether anybody liked him or not.

In 1925 the Ford Motor Company paid its employees wages amounting to $250,000,000, and Henry called attention to the fact that while wages since 1913 had more than doubled, the price of his cars had decreased 40 per cent. A Ford car cost less per pound than beef steak. Everybody bought a Ford—if they weren't buying a Chevrolet or some higher-priced car. America was riding on wheels, mostly Ford wheels, and some doctors were pointing out that if this sort of thing continued to increase it would be only a question of time when Americans lost the use of their legs. In time legs might become vestigial elements, like the small vertebrae at the base of the spine which are said to be the remnants of a tail that our ancestors wore with gay abandon in those halcyon days when they swung from trees.

Chapter Twenty-seven

In December 1925, a startled world learned that Henry Ford had gone in for a bit of the higher culture, and was paying attention to the lighter side of life. In the new laboratory building at Dearborn he had set aside a section to be used as a ballroom and had invited the neighbours in for a barn dance.

After his early years in Detroit he had come back to live in the old homestead, and by this time had erected a mansion on the family acres. He had gone in heavily for farming, using tractors and all the latest improvements. He was a gentleman farmer on a large scale, doing it purely for the love of the thing, but managing to make the farm pay. Now he was reviving one of the sociable features of farm life of his boyhood days.

Champion fiddlers were present at the dance, playing the old-time favourites: "Pop Goes the Weasel", "Fisher's Hornpipe", "Arkansas Traveller", "Old Zip Coon", "Lady Washington's Reel", and many others, long forgotten.

"The old dances are coming back," Henry told inquiring reporters. "In fact, they're here. We're simply falling into line." A repertoire of old dances was being taught at the Dearborn laboratory two nights a week. Everyone had to learn to dance correctly, and to help them do it Henry got out a dance manual as simple as the manual that accompanied his car. It was standardized, too. Twenty-one different quadrilles were scientifically analysed—presumably by Ford quadrille analysers—and four were found to embody the best features. The other seventeen were junked, in the best Ford tradition, and the teaching was simplified and standardized to these favoured four. "What we are trying to do with dances is to standardize them," Ford told the amazed reporters. They hadn't the least doubt that he could do it.

What was Henry up to now?—everybody wanted to know. Was there no limit to what he could set his mind on in off hours when he wasn't turning out Fords?

Apparently there was none. In 1923 he had purchased the Wayside Inn, at Sudbury, Mass., the setting of Longfellow's *Tales of a Wayside Inn*. He also purchased the blacksmith shop of Caleb Taft in Uxbridge, Mass., built in 1787. This was the shop under the spreading chestnut tree where Longfellow's blacksmith had stood—to the annoyance of small boys who had to recite the poem in school, thoroughly fed up with Longfellow and his blacksmith, too.

Then, between periods of dancing gaily old barn dance numbers, Henry purchased the old Everett mansion in Charlestown where Daniel Webster had stayed when he came to Boston to dedicate the monument on Bunker Hill.

It was announced—mistakenly, as it turned out—that Henry had offered to buy the Statue of Liberty. But he did buy the little country school at Sterling, Mass., the school to which Mary's little lamb had followed her, to the annoyance of succeeding generations of first-graders, who had to memorize the doggerel.

For some time, while Henry attended the weekly dances at Dearborn and plugged industriously for public support of old-style dancing, the country wondered what he was up to, for he kept on buying other antiques and shipping them to Dearborn. Some said that he was starting a museum, while others averred that it was only Henry in quest of his youth. He had done so much to destroy old-time America, they said, that it was only natural that, now he was growing old, he should want to gather souvenirs of his youth around him.

As a matter of fact, Henry was growing younger, not older. He had spent practically no part of his life in play. Now he had the means and the time to play. So he was playing and amusing himself, in his own quaint way. The fact that he wanted to leave a huge museum of early Americana to the American people seems merely incidental.

As production mounted at River Rouge, the collection of antiques also mounted. The newspapers reported the purchases with growing wonder. An old fire-fighting hand-drawn ladder truck and bucket truck and hose reel from Plymouth arrived at the same time as a hansom cab of the 1870's, said to have carried Lillian Russell.

Then there came a Rogers locomotive of 1860 that had seen service during the Civil War; wooden water pipes laid in 1797; early American drawing-room furniture; an 1850 boiler; a decaying rowboat a century old; drugstore furnishings of the nineties; five stage coaches that dated from 1804 to 1859; an 1823 oxcart; the tools and laboratory equipment from the workshop in Florida where Thomas A. Edison had developed the modern incandescent lamp; a sawmill from Michigan; and several antique engines.

In an unending stream the relics of a century poured into Dearborn: hooked rugs, wheat flails, Conestoga wagons, gristmills, cider presses, cotton gins from the old South, and moss-covered buckets that hung in some well, long since caved in. Henry Ford was collecting souvenirs of the old America that he, more than any other man or any group of men, had done the most to change. For it was the motor-car and roads that had changed America; and industrialization and mass production that had made the change inevitable. And Henry was the high prophet of mass production.

Just as he had led the way into the motor age, so he was to lead the parade of collectors of antiques that began to scour every bypath in search of old furniture, old crockery, old spinning wheels, old hooked rugs, even kitchen furniture. Henry Ford had set a pattern and an army of collectors of antique and near-antique furniture and bric-à-brac followed at his heels. They bought anything and everything that looked old, as long as they could buy it at an old farmhouse.

Antique dealers from New York obligingly filled hundreds of farmhouses with antiques—many of them made a month before, and aged by acids. Some were properly worm-eaten— by a machine that made a hundred wormholes a minute. The furniture was displayed on worn old hooked rugs—made in modern factories and "aged" by acids, rubbing machines, and plain dirt. Every rural village soon had its "Ye Olde An-. tique Shoppe", and farmhouses along a thousand roads, espe- cially in New England, had weatherworn signs telling passing motorists—most of them in Model T's—that antiques were for sale within. Every such house and "shoppe" had an old spin- ning wheel in front of it.

Naturally, there were many genuine antiques among the car- loads of modern production. Some knew the genuine from the imitation. But what did it matter whether it was old or not, if it looked old? Few knew the difference, anyhow. Henry Ford had inadvertently set a fashion, and people were following it— even the Metropolitan Museum in New York, which collected a lot of old furniture it had owned for years and put it in an "American Wing" to show how earlier generations of Ameri- cans had lived. In its first eight months, a quarter of a million people flocked into that wing.

While Henry was collecting antiques all over the country to fill his Dearborn Museum, the Ford Motor Company collected 199 specimens of marine antiques—old cargo vessels bought from the United States Shipping Board. These old freighters that had carried war cargoes to Europe and all over the world were no longer needed and were sold to Ford for their value as junk—$1,697,470. They were towed up the coast to the St. Lawrence River, through the Great Lakes, and so to River Rouge, where they were scrapped by a force of 1,500 men. Within a few weeks after their arrival—sometimes within a few days—steel from those ships would be coming off the produc- tion line as part of a Model T Ford. It was wonderful to specu- late that some part of your Ford might have ploughed the seas, and even had a German torpedo sent against it.

There had been changes in the Model T during these years after the war—81 in all, including an entirely new body shape and hood. These changes cost the Ford Motor Company some

$8,000,000 for material, labour, and engineering, without counting time lost from production. The new Model T was a better car than ever—and not quite so homely-looking. It had need to be. The Chevrolet was catching up, and other cars at higher prices were attracting the public's dollars. Increasing numbers of Ford owners were trading in their old cars, not for new Fords, but for something that looked better, even if it cost more. By 1925 the writing was on the wall, but Henry refused to see it. While competing cars were coming out in all the colours of the rainbow, Henry still was painting his black.

Chapter Twenty-eight

BY the first months of 1926 there were eighty-six Ford plants and branches scattered all over the globe. Fifty-two were in the United States, thirty-four in other countries. The plants' capacity was over two million cars a year.

Precision manufacturing by automatic machines turned out parts accurate to within two ten-thousandths of an inch. They were interchangeable with a similar part on any Ford anywhere around the globe.

As subsidiary enterprises, all of them leading directly to the production of the Model T, Ford was engaged in mining coal, cutting timber, distilling alcohol from wood, developing water power, building electric locomotives, making machines for making parts, making gauges, growing flax, rolling steel, making glass, and running a railroad. He was a busy man.

Production had reached such an efficient point that a Ford ore boat could dock at River Rouge in the morning, its cargo be unloaded, dumped into blast furnaces, reduced to iron, cast in moulds, and by afternoon be part of a Ford engine, which might be installed right away in a Ford chassis, and run off the production line before the whistle blew at five o'clock.

It was said that the captain of one of Henry's ore carriers left his ship one morning for a trip to Detroit. By mistake, the wrecking crew that was dismantling old war emergency freighters seized the ore boat, cut it up, sent it to the blast furnaces—and at five o'clock when the captain came back he saw the rejuvenated remnants of his 10,000-ton steamer leaving the factory gates in the form of thousands of saucy Model T's.

This was one of the last of the Ford jokes, but it had its basis in solid fact. The principle of fast production had become so advanced that the company never found it necessary to keep more than a ten-day supply of raw materials on hand.

Everything was used, nothing wasted. Eighty million pounds of steel that once had gone into scrap each year were used to make smaller parts. Bolts, nuts, everything that fell to the floor was swept up and sorted by automatic machines. Rags, paper, and bits of wood found a useful function to perform—even if only to supply heat.

The motor age that was born in the early 1900's had come of age in the twenties, and by its own vigour had boomed the production of oil, steel, leather, and a hundred other commodities. Of petrol and oil, two billion dollars' worth a year flowed into the tanks of American cars. A billion dollars a year went into building new roads and modernizing old ones. Still, on a week-end, there were not enough roads. The traffic line had come to stay; and the traffic cop had become a national institution.

By the mid-twenties America had become style-conscious, colour-conscious, gadget-conscious. The automobile industry fell into line with other industries, giving the public each year something new, something more stylish, more colourful.

It began in 1925, when the staid blues and blacks gave way to green, yellow, red, brown, tan, and fifty colours in between. At the annual automobile show for 1926 more than fifty colours of body were on display. And they were stylish bodies, too.

Others than Ford had learned the details of mass production; engineers working for General Motors were as knowing as those working for Ford. Other companies could develop or purchase machines and machine tools just as efficient as those used by Ford. He had led the way, but they had followed, and had added ideas of their own.

K

By 1926 Henry had only one great advantage over other automobile manufacturers: he produced only one model, in huge numbers, so he could sell cheaper than anyone else. Nobody in the automobile world could beat Henry at that. So they didn't try. They built something different and better-looking, and produced it in numbers great enough to permit selling it at a low price—even if not as low as that of a Model T.

"Colour, body-line, beauty", were featured in the advertisements—and Henry overlooked or never had learned that it is the women of America, rather than the men, who do the buying, even of the family car. Henry was selling plain transportation, while the wives of America now were buying style in motor-cars—at only a slightly higher price.

Early in 1926 it was rumoured that soon Henry would change the style of his car and bring out something that looked more like the high-priced cars. And they would come out in colour, too.

But it was only a rumour; it was denied by the Ford Motor Company, which said, "It is an absolute policy that no change may be made which cannot be incorporated into any existing car". The rumours persisted that Ford would change. But the denials always squelched the rumours. There was the Model T, its parts interchangeable and changeless, the cheapest car in the world. You could have it in any colour—as long as it was black. Take it or leave it!

The public left it. They left it as suddenly and as eagerly as they had embraced it. The production of two million cars a year during 1923 to 1925 fell off sharply in 1926. It slowed down in the summer, slowed further in the autumn. While Ford distributors everywhere pleaded for a change, Henry sat mum—and sales fell and continued to fall, week after week.

In February 1927, Henry announced that, "no drastic change of any kind is contemplated". Ford dealers groaned and looked around their salesrooms at unsold Fords, complete with their old-fashioned transmission systems, their clattering little engines, their bouncy springs, their built-in rattles. Nearly fifteen million of them were on the roads, but nobody wanted any more of them. They wanted something different, something that looked a lot better, even if they had to pay more for it.

Three months later the fifteen millionth Ford Model T rolled off the line. Nobody cared—except Henry. He could keep it as a souvenir, for nobody wanted it. It was too homely, too old-fashioned, and there were just too many exactly like it. It was a standardized product—and Americans were individualists now as to motor-cars. They had left the stout-hearted little Model T behind them.

Chapter Twenty-nine

THE fifteen millionth Ford marked the end of an era. Next day the Ford Company announced that it would abandon the Model T and bring out a completely different car as soon as possible. All Ford factories, except those still making spare parts for Model T's, were shut down so that the entire plant could be reorganized to produce the new car, which was only in the design stage.

This announcement, after a year of reiterated denials that Ford would change his model, was as much of a surprise to the automobile industry and the public as was their bewilderment over the fact that he hadn't announced the change a year ago. Everybody but Henry knew that Model T was dying, and had known it for eighteen months. Had only Henry been blind?

There was much speculation about Henry. Some pointed out that he was an old man now—he was sixty-four—and suggested that his mind was failing. Others remarked that he was as stubborn as a mule, would let nobody dictate to him, not even his customers, and certainly not his dealers. Still others said that the cost of the change-over would be so great that perhaps Henry thought it better to continue selling Model T's in reduced numbers, rather than scrap most of the machinery in his plant.

Nobody but Henry knew the answer, and he never told. He

was at least a year, perhaps two years late in coming to a decision. Actually, the decision had been taken out of his hands by the buying public. For once in his life—for the first and the last time—Henry Ford had been dictated to by the great master of all industry—the buying public. By not buying, they told him flatly that he could either bring out a new model, or go out of business.

The average citizen, who treasures the belief that he runs things in this democracy, can take heart from the fact that he really did run Henry Ford for a brief period. If Henry realized that—as he probably did—he never admitted it publicly. It was likely a sore point with him, and may have made him wonder if he was slipping. If he was, he soon got his feet in the grit and pounded ahead with his old-time vigour.

Changing over to a new model meant scrapping twenty thousand expensive machines which had been designed solely to turn out parts for an automobile of which nobody wanted another copy. It also meant rebuilding and changing some twenty thousand other machines. It meant changing plants all over the world as well as at Highland Park and River Rouge, and replanning the intricate and finely adjusted conveyor systems that brought each part to an appointed place at an appointed moment.

It meant building the first model car, testing it, tearing it apart, breaking every individual part to ascertain the strength of it. Two hundred engineers laboured on the car, another two hundred worked to design machinery to build it. The cost of all this labour, and new machinery for production before a single car was produced except by hand labour, was to be over a hundred million dollars. During it all, Henry never lost his placidity. He examined every detail with a shrewd eye, in which a smile often twinkled. Apparently nothing could get the old man down.

River Rouge was decided upon as the main factory, replacing Highland Park, which was to continue making parts for the millions of Model T's still on the roads, and still to be on the roads for years to come. In making his new car, Henry wasn't for a moment going to let his old Model T customers down—he wanted those cars of his to run until they had given the owner every ounce of service that he had built into them.

That was a kind of honesty peculiar to Henry Ford—and to few other men in industry. If he had left the Model T an orphan, with no new parts for it, he might have built up within a few months or years a tremendous market for his new model. But Henry's mind didn't run in that channel. He'd stick by the people who had stuck by him. Until the last Model T had gasped its last, Henry was right there behind it, with new parts to keep it going another 20,000 miles. This was service, and Henry had dedicated his life to service. He was making good on his word.

There was tremendous activity at River Rouge, where turbo-generators were set up to produce 250,000 horse power—double the amount of the plant in the previous year. Presses that weighed 200,000 pounds were replaced by presses of 500,000 pounds. Machinery that could have been changed was in many cases sold or thrown on the junk heap, because more efficient machinery could be designed and built. New buildings were erected, and thirty miles of new conveyor system were installed in a plant that covered two square miles at River Rouge. Like changes were going forward in Ford plants all over the world.

Meanwhile, speculation, as they say, was rife. Reporters from newspapers all over the nation descended upon River Rouge to discover and flash to their papers the latest word about what Henry was doing. And this in itself was a remarkable thing, for any other automobile manufacturer in America could change his model at any time, and nobody cared a hoot what new contraption he was bringing out. But Henry was different. He was news. Everything he did or was going to do was news. He, himself, was what reporters called a natural for publicity.

So they tried to get into the factory, and they asked workmen what they were doing, and what the new Ford looked like, and so on. They even donned overalls and tried to get in for a look around. After they were thrown out, they went back to their hotels and sent rumours to their papers.

Dispatches from these news-hounds declared that the new car was to be a cross between the Lincoln and the Ford. Henry had bought the Lincoln factory in 1922 and had been turning out the highest-priced car in America in the Lincoln plant.

Henry said nothing. Why should he, when obliging reporters

were keeping the newspapers filled with free Ford publicity at a time when he hadn't a single new car to sell? But he must have enjoyed many a smile at the curiosity and the gullibility of humans. Henry was not without a sense of humour, though he seldom gave an outward demonstration of it.

By August the public heard from its news sleuths that the new Ford was in existence; it had been seen scooting along the roads around Dearborn with Henry at the wheel. But it was disguised, they said, under an old Model T body. Later, the public learned that a strange-looking small car was to be seen daily on the roads of Wayne County, tearing along at anything up to a hundred miles an hour. Ford officials squashed this by an announcement that the car was a Ford, but not THE Ford—it was just one of several experimental models.

Whoever ran the publicity campaign was a genius—there is no doubt that some publicity expert in the Ford organization was pulling the strings. Maybe it was Henry himself. Nobody knows. But by one device after another, public interest was aroused to a high point. What it all boiled down to was free publicity on a scale unprecedented in any business.

Then it was announced by the Ford company that the new Ford had been seen, but only by high Ford officials. They had been permitted to peek only in "the semi-privacy of the final assembly building, the doors of which were carefully guarded".

It was also reported that the car again was being driven by Mr. Ford himself—not a reasonable facsimile—"but only be-hind high fences within the Ford plant".

This new Ford was so wonderful that nobody could be per-mitted to see it until it was officially born, and ready for delivery to panting prospective owners. Henry—or somebody who worked for him—knew the American public. All you have to do to an American is to tell him he can't see something, and he'll yearn to see it. Public expectancy was aroused to the boiling point—and, what is more important, the buying point.

News of the car was fed out by degrees. By thoughtfully leaving a part of the walls unguarded, a photographer was al-lowed to get a picture of the new Ford. He probably thought he was smart, but he was only being used by Henry's clever publicists.

The New York *Post* published the picture, claiming it as the first picture of the new Ford car, snapped in a moment when its guards were out for lunch. Later on, other pictures appeared, snapped on the roads of Michigan, which by this time were lined with photographers, all hoping to catch the elusive Ford. It looked like any other small car. But the public thought it must be something wonderful—which was the basic idea of the whole publicity campaign.

Every day new pictures appeared in the newspapers. All of them were supposed to have been taken surreptitiously, by bold photographers who had been skulking for days and weeks in the hedgerows of Michigan just to get this shot. Actually, most of the pictures, if not all of them, had been handed out by Henry's publicity department.

Finally, the campaign reached a climax. On December 1, 1927, the Ford Motor Company started a five-day series of full-page advertisements in 2,000 newspapers from coast to coast, announcing the new car. It paid $1,300,000 for those adverments. That was only fair, to give the newspapers something. They had given Henry Ford maybe as much as $10,000,000 worth of free publicity, under the guise of news. They should be permitted to get something back through the advertising department.

On October 20 the first Model A rolled off the assembly line, and on December 2 there was a nationwide showing of the new car. It had been shipped sewed up in canvas so nobody could get a peek at it before the appointed moment.

New York greeted the new Ford with as much enthusiasm and noise as it displayed to a visiting celebrity. At three o'clock in the morning curious New Yorkers began to gather in front of the Ford showroom at 1710 Broadway, and by nine o'clock police on duty were calling for the reserves to keep the crowd moving. Naturally, it didn't move, and everything stayed stuck all day. As the New York *World* reported, "Excitement could hardly have been greater had Pah-wah, the sacred white elephant of Burma, elected to sit for seven days on the flagpole of the Woolworth Building".

The Ford people hired Madison Square Garden that afternoon, and threw up barricades around their showrooms all over the country to keep the plate glass intact. Buses brought visitors to New York and the Stock Exchange went up like a skyrocket. Everybody was optimistic. Henry had come through triumphantly! "Good old Henry!" people said.

In Detroit 100,000 visitors stormed the showrooms. Mounted police were called to control the mob in Cleveland; immense Kansas City Convention Hall was jammed with curious people. All over the nation the crowds congregated, and tens of thousands left orders for delivery when possible.

The Model A bore no family resemblance to its predecessor. It had a modern, stylish body-shape, standard gearshift, a roomy, comfortably upholstered interior, and the bodies were painted in a variety of colours, including Niagara Blue, Dawn Grey, and Arabian Sand—which were blue, grey, and tan before the advertising department thought up those new names. And you could still have it painted black.

Before December 1, customers had filed orders for 400,000 Fords they had never seen. After they saw it, additional hundreds of thousands of orders were signed—with a down payment. Production was speeded up rapidly, and before a year went by the daily production rate was 6,000 cars a day, and the number of employees was 186,000. Henry was out of the woods, and beginning to get back part of the hundred millions the change had cost him.

Those who had wondered if Henry was slipping were answered by Ford himself in July 1927. "Sixty-four today," he said, "and the biggest job of my life ahead of me." At a time of life when most men are thinking of retiring, Henry was just getting his second wind!

Busy as he was, running a great industrial empire, Henry Ford found time for outside activities, prominent among which was his interest in the education of boys for industry.

He had never been in sympathy with the trade school as it was commonly organized, for he felt that boys got only a smattering of knowledge in such institutions and had no practical opportunity to use that knowledge. So the Henry Ford Trade School was incorporated in 1916, to aid boys whose circumstances compelled them to leave school early.

There were three basic principles: the boy—from twelve to

eighteen years of age—was to be kept a boy and not changed
into a working man until his schooling was over; academic
training went hand in hand with practical industrial instruc-
tion; and to give a boy pride in his work, he was trained in
making articles that were to be used in the production of Ford
cars. He was paid for such work.

When the boys graduate, they may work for Ford or go elsewhere. Most of them work for Ford, because they do not know
where better jobs, with more opportunity for advancement,
may be found. "There is no string tied to the boys," Henry
declared. "They have earned their own way and are under obli-
gations to no one. There is no charity. The place pays for itself."
His attitude towards the boys in his trade school showed Henry
Ford in one of his most engaging lights. He had never forgotten
that he started as a hard-working boy, with little education. He
wanted to make it easier for boys of the new generation—and
he did.

The Ford Hospital in Detroit was started on somewhat similar lines, with Henry, as usual, paying the bills. He didn't set
out deliberately to build a hospital, but made a subscription to
the fund for a Detroit General Hospital, designed to be erected
by popular subscription. Long before the first buildings were
finished, the funds became exhausted, and Henry was called
upon for another subscription. He refused to contribute, because he felt that the managers of the project should have known
how much the building was going to cost before they started it.
He had no confidence in such management, so he offered to
take over the whole hospital, paying back all the subscriptions
that had been made. It was a characteristic Ford move—Henry
didn't care for partners, especially unbusinesslike ones.

The hospital was turned over to Ford who, on August 1, 1918,
turned the whole institution over to the government, and it became General Hospital No. 36, housing 1,500 patients. It was
returned to Henry in October 1919, and on November 10 the
first private patient was admitted.

Henry had definite ideas about hospitals, as he had about
everything else. In general, he didn't think highly of hospitals,
and declared that it wasn't at all certain whether hospitals exist
for patients or for doctors. "There seems to be a notion," he

said, "that a patient, and especially when in a hospital, becomes the property of the doctor. A conscientious practitioner does not exploit the patient. A less conscientious one does. Many physicians seem to regard the sustaining of their own diagnoses as of as great moment as the recovery of the patient."

In his new hospital, Henry got away from all that by having a "closed" hospital. All physicians and nurses were employed by the hospital, and could have no private practice outside of it. The doctors were selected with care, and were paid salaries that amounted to as much as they could earn in private practice. Thus, the doctors had no financial interest in any patient—who could not be treated by any other doctor from outside. His own doctor could not co-operate. If he was sick enough to go to the Ford hospital, the patient put himself on a sort of standardized Ford rehabilitation line, with Ford employees working on him.

Born and raised on a farm, Henry Ford never lost interest in farming and in country life. Actually, he never became a city man, never lived in a city after his early years. He went back to Dearborn and farming, as a change from his industrial activities. By 1932, he had 12,000 acres under cultivation on his experimental farm, two-thirds of it devoted to soybeans, of which the yearly harvest was 100,000 bushels. It was Henry's way of linking farming and industry, for some finished parts for Ford cars —the steering wheel, for one—are made from a plastic material produced from soybeans after the oil is extracted.

Henry suggested that a farmer might till the soil in summer, work in a factory in winter. He worked towards a combination of farm and factory by decentralizing his own industry, and setting up little factories in farming communities. One, at Northville, near Detroit, makes only valves. It is a small factory, but it makes a great many valves, almost entirely by machinery. Any farmer can work in that factory, for the skill is in the machines. Then, during the growing and harvesting season, he goes back to his farm.

Suppose we all moved outdoors every spring and summer and lived the wholesome life of the outdoors for three or four months (Henry suggested). We could not have slack times. The farm has its dull season. That is the time for the farmer to come into the factory and help produce the things he needs to till the farm. The factory also has its dull season. That is the time for the workmen to go out to the land to help produce food. Thus we might take the slack out of work and restore the balance between the artificial and the natural.

He did what he could to help bring these conditions about. At Flat Rock, fifteen miles from Detroit, he dammed a river. The dam also served as a bridge for the Detroit, Toledo & Ironton Railway, and a road for the public, all in the one construction. Damming the river gave enough water power to run a hydro-electric plant for his small factory there. Nearly all the workers had farms or plots of ground in the vicinity, so they worked their farms and they worked for Henry, in healthful country surroundings. It was a combination of agriculture and industrialism that made nobody happier than it did Henry, who had the genius and the means to bring it into being.

The children of Dearborn's primary schools were encouraged to grow gardens, forty by sixty feet each. The ground was ploughed, harrowed, seeded, and turned over to them, with tools made to their size. Men working in the factories could share in the co-operative farming on Ford's thousands of acres, and grow their own food.

Henry believed that eventually industry would be decentralized, and that in time people would cease crowding together in big cities. He thought that the big city had served its purpose and that eventually people would spread out over the country. "A great city is really a helpless mass," he said. "Everything it uses is carried to it. Stop transport and the city stops. It lives off the shelves of stores. The shelves produce nothing. The city cannot feed, clothe, warm, or house itself. City conditions of work and living are so artificial that instincts rebel against their unnaturalness."

Henry practised what he preached, and made it possible for thousands of men in his small plants to live healthful lives in country, to work outdoors in the summer, to work in a factory during the slack farming season.

He took a look at the Mississippi River, and was struck by the waste of so much water power. The Mississippi valley was without coal, he noted, and people had to pay high prices to have it hauled to them from hundreds of miles away. And all the time, there was the great river, with millions of units of unused hydro-electric horse power, flowing past their doors. Henry wondered why they didn't harness it, as he had harnessed the Rouge River. He pointed out that, for nothing beyond the initial cost, they could heat, light, cook, and work with electricity. He was amazed that they hadn't done something about it.

Chapter Thirty

Henry found time to spare from building automobiles to interest himself in air transportation. His interest at first was intense, but eventually he was to come to the conclusion that the airplane was 90 per cent man and 10 per cent machine, which was an unsafe basis. Undoubtedly that was a fair estimate during the 1920's, but in the past twenty years the aircraft industry has whittled down the percentage of man's proneness to err and has increased the safety factor of the machine itself.

Henry and his son Edsel made it plain that there was no intention of the Ford Motor Company to go into the airplane business on a large scale, but only to further its development by providing a landing field at Dearborn as an incentive to those working on metal airplane and airship construction in Detroit.

Henry backed a Detroit-Chicago-Cleveland air express service by guaranteeing a two-thousand-pound load of Ford parts for each trip. It didn't pay, but Henry had fun. He would stand around on the flying field and talk to the pilots. He was past sixty then, but so receptive and alert was his mind that within a few months it was evident that he knew more about aviation from the business end than most of the veteran pilots he was talking to. They knew flying, but Henry knew costs—down to a fraction of a cent a pound.

He decided to learn something about manufacturing airplanes, so in 1925 he built a factory on the Dearborn Airport for the Stout Metal Airplane Company, whose president was William B. Stout, a brilliant aeronautical engineer, who had produced the Stout monoplane powered by a Liberty engine. Henry bought that company in 1925 and made it a division of the Ford Motor Company.

It was his delight to talk to commercial pilots when they flew in to Dearborn; and Henry was of as great interest to them as they were to him. It was during these years of his aviation interest that I met Henry.

He was then sixty-three, but didn't look a day over fifty; and he had the eager enthusiasm of a youth. He was of medium height and had a very slender figure. His hair was white, worn long, brushed back from his forehead. When he talked to you, he would lean forward slightly and gaze directly into your eyes. His eyes were grey-green and very sharp-looking, and you got the impression that he was sizing you up, and not coming to a very flattering conclusion about you.

He was very democratic, very plain in his speech, put on no airs, never threw his weight about. And yet I gained the impression that he felt superior to the people around him—as, indeed, he was! It has become an accepted fiction in the United States that "all men are created equal". Quite obviously they are not—there are weak men, strong men, tall men, short men, brilliant men, and stupid men. Most of us don't feel equal to the next man—except maybe politically, in that we each have one vote.

On one occasion I recall that he asked me what I thought about the all-metal dirigible. An opinionated young man, I at once said that I didn't think it was any good—as a veteran airplane pilot I naturally held lighter-than-air in no great regard. Henry looked at me sternly.

"No good?" he repeated, questioningly. "Humph!"

He gazed at me for maybe half a minute, while I held my ground and stared back at him, and then, without another word, he turned abruptly and walked away. I felt slightly foolish. But he had asked my opinion, and I had given it to him.

About a week later I again landed at the Dearborn Airport—I was flying for the B. F. Goodrich Rubber Company at the time, and often had to carry their sales executives from Akron to Detroit. Henry was on hand, as usual, and wandered over to the plane as I got out.

"How do you do, Mr. Ford," I said. "Nice day."

"So you think the metal dirigible is no good, do you?" he asked at once, leaning towards me with his usual slight stoop and his sharp look.

"No good at all, Mr. Ford," I said. He glared at me for maybe half a minute, as though he could stare me into changing my mind. I wondered that he had even remembered our conversation—such as it was!—for he met so many people, most of them important.

"You're sure it's no good?" he asked again.

"Not worth the powder to blow it up," I replied firmly. "It can't do anything that an airplane can't do better and faster—and airplanes don't leak."

This time he didn't even say, "Humph!" He just walked away from me without a word or a grunt. I met him two or three times after that, and he never again brought up the subject of that metal dirigible.

But he did discuss his mooring mast, then in process of erection. "How do you like our mooring mast?" he asked one day, when I had brought the Goodrich sales manager over from Akron and was awaiting his return for Detroit.

"It's a nice mast, if you want to go in for that sort of thing," I said.

"What sort of thing?" asked Henry.

"The antique business, Mr. Ford," I replied. "Balloons are antiques—haven't you noticed?"

"They're nothing of the sort," he said at once. "They're the only safe thing for over-ocean transport. If the engines all stop, they stay up, at any rate."

"But they're not going any place in a hurry," I said, "even with all engines running. Someone has sold you a pup, Mr. Ford—that mooring mast is an antique. You can put it in your museum."

Chapter Thirty-one

HENRY'S experience with aviation was, on the whole, very unrewarding. In the mid-twenties he was very Zeppelin-conscious.

Airplane pilots as a rule thought that the huge Zeppelins built in Germany and the American versions built by the Goodyear Tyre & Rubber Company at Akron were rather like dinosaurs, at least as compared with airplanes. And so it turned out—they are now extinct, except for their small progeny, the non-rigids, a sort of vestigial remnant of the huge rigids, called blimps, because that seems to be the natural thing to call them.

Henry thought they were going places. And airplane pilots, to a man, disagreed with him and told him so. One of them, after a talk about Zeppelins, said to Ford, "Henry, you're slipping. You want to watch it—you may be going nuts." Then he grinned and walked away—turning the tables on Henry, who liked to walk away himself.

Henry looked after him, rather baffled. Then he turned to me. "I don't like that fellow," he said. "He's too opinionated." Henry never thought that he was opinionated. But he certainly had strong opinions on the use of alcohol.

"Alcohol is a poison," he said to one of his biographers, who

quoted him. "I know that the human system can absorb just
that much without getting hurt." He held up his little finger to
show how much. "I would like to have people know that. But
I don't want anyone to stop drinking because I tell them to."
But when the Eighteenth Amendment was adopted, he felt that
he was on firm ground. He would employ no person known to
drink or to have liquor in his possession. Large numbers of Ford
employees drank, on principle, largely to assert themselves as
individuals. But if Henry found out, they were fired.

Aviation apparently fascinated Henry Ford, and he tried to
do something about it. In the Stout-designed Ford trimotor he
had a plane that would carry a big pay load, for those days, at
minimum cost.

But he seemed to lose interest in any further development of
those planes—the last one, that came off the production line in
1931 was pretty much like the first one. In a business that was
moving fast, Henry was standing still.

The factory continued to experiment with a four-engined
plane which would carry forty passengers, but Henry didn't
favour it. They had built a bomber in 1929 which didn't have
Henry's entire approval, but he let the development go forward.
It crashed on a test flight in November 1930, killing the test
pilot and the chief test mechanic. Mr. Ford, who couldn't
resign himself to the idea that test pilots were expendable,
withdrew from the combat plane field.

Two years earlier he had been saddened by the loss of another
pilot, Harry Brooks, a young man who joined the Ford airplane
division because his father, Joseph Brooks was a member, an
old-time fiddler who was a great friend of Henry's. By 1926
young Brooks was chief test pilot for Ford, and had tested a
small single-seater of his own design, built by Ford's airplane
division, under the direction of Pop Mayo.

That plane and a second one were successful. Young Brooks
established a record for distance for planes in that class—flying
nearly one thousand miles on fifty gallons of petrol. A few days
later, flying down the Florida coast, he dropped into the ocean.
His body was never found. Although Henry said that he would
continue to develop the small plane, he soon gave it up. His
heart wasn't in the work.

In 1936 he experimented briefly with a small plane built around the V-8 motor—an impractical idea, considering the weight of the automobile engine and the cost of converting it to airplane use, and at a period when small engines, especially designed for aircraft, were available, though at greater cost. The plane created little interest and was not produced commercially.

In 1941 he announced that his company was experimenting with a two-seater "which we expect to put on the market ultimately", adding that the new plane would probably combine the features of an ordinary type plane and the autogiro—about the neatest trick of the decade, if he could pull it off.

"We are just beginning to go places in aviation," he said. But he never went anywhere in particular until the last war, when he produced Liberator bombers at his Willow Run bomber plant. And the Liberator wasn't a Ford development.

It is strange that, with the practically unlimited resources at his command, and with enough money and prestige to attract the most brilliant aeronautical brains of the country to his banner, Henry Ford made almost no contribution to the progress of aviation after the era of the Ford trimotor.

The explanation seems to be that Henry never became thoroughly sold on aviation—certainly not to the extent that he was sold on the automobile. It was a side line, an interesting hobby, something to experiment with.

In 1928 he had told the Associated Press that he was "strong for air travel and would take a plane whenever necessary to get anywhere". But his one experience with air travel had been in 1927, when he had a brief flight with Colonel Charles A. Lindbergh. After that, he evidently never found it necessary to get anywhere by airplane, for there is no record of his being up since then.

Chapter Thirty-two

A YEAR after the introduction of the Model A, production was at a rate of 6,000 cars a day and over 186,000 men were on the pay roll. By 1929, when the business boom had reached its height, Model A had taken the lead in the sales of cars. Henry had got back his hundred million and was riding high again.

When the stock market crash of 1929 staggered the nation and values were falling everywhere, Henry's response was to keep on spending, and on December 1 he announced an increase of the minimum wage to $7.00 a day.

As Henry had predicted long before, better machines had not displaced men; they had given men more and more jobs, at better wages, and without backbreaking drudgery. In 1910 no workman could own one of the cars he had helped to build. Now almost any workman could, and usually did, own one. The used-car market had made personal transportation available to the masses.

The year 1930 saw stock values continuing to dwindle until they were fifty billion dollars below the boom peak of 1929. But Ford, the chronic optimist, was untroubled. He made large investments in the Brazil rubber fields, began experiments

making synthetic rubber, reorganized his factories in foreign countries, selling part of the stock—but not a controlling interest!—to citizens of those countries.

"We retain the control of each company," he said, "only so that it may be managed in accordance with our fundamental principles and have the benefit of our engineering experience. We are not at all interested merely in floating a number of automobile companies in Europe or anywhere else in the world. But we believe that our industrial policies move towards the end of creating consuming power, raising the standards of living, and thus diminishing poverty. In this belief we may be right or again we may be wrong—we believe that our experience has proved we are right." Nobody doubted that Henry was right most of the time—maybe 90 per cent of the time, perhaps as much as 99 per cent.

In England the Ford plant at Dagenham was planned to be the second largest in the world, to manufacture cars for Great Britain, Ireland, and some parts of the British Empire. Other plants, some for manufacture, others for assembly of parts, were scattered all over the world: Buenos Aires, Montevideo, São Paulo, Mexico City; Santiago, Chile; Yokohama, Japan; Germany, France, Holland, Belgium. These were all separate companies, with stock held by citizens of the various countries, but control firmly held in Dearborn.

By the end of 1930 it was evident that the depression was more than a big dent in the national economy. It began to look like a very deep hole of unemployment into which millions were tumbling. Meanwhile Henry was putting his best optimistic foot forward, and saying that bad management, not vague outside forces, was the cause of the business slump. Proper leadership would effect economies and thus lower prices so that people could buy. He blamed the speculative mania of the twenties for the nation's troubles, but towards the end of 1931 Ford sales had fallen off, and Henry felt impelled to reduce his basic wage; but the Model A still was going strong. The twenty millionth Ford rolled off the line, with four years of technical improvements in its construction. It was larger, slightly heavier, with a longer wheel base, lower hung chassis, and practically no rattles for the first year of its life.

This Ford No. 20,000,000 made a triumphal tour of the United States and was greeted by local celebrations everywhere, and while political disturbances all over the world increased, while business continued its downward trend and unemployment mounted, Henry calmly announced one day in February that he intended to manufacture an eight-cylinder car but would continue to make the four-cylinder Model A.

Then one morning in March he ordered all production stopped immediately. He had decided that something drastic had to be done, and he was doing it. The hundred million dollars he had spent in the development of Model A had served its purpose, he declared. It was to be regarded only as an investment in experience. He had said some years before, "The only thing certain in life is change, and when a man gets too old to change, why then he dies." Henry had no intention of shuffling off. At sixty-nine he was still as full of zest as ever.

"We are going to keep prices down so that the public can buy our cars," he said, in reply to a question about the public's buying power. "We shall continue to make the four-cylinder model. The eight is only two fours, you know."

Henry had been interested in an eight-cylinder engine since 1921, had been experimenting for the past year and had several models on test when he decided on the change.

The Ford V-8 was a handsome car, offered in fourteen different body styles—all of them stylish, and in a wide variety of colours.

Features were an automatic spark, synchronized gearshift, a double-drop frame, rustless steel, and rubber mountings at many places to eliminate rattles—hitherto a standard Ford feature. The public had demonstrated that it wanted luxury and comfort, and no rattles; so Henry was supplying the demand.

But he still had his stubborn streak. He brought out the car with mechanical brakes, when everyone was clamouring for hydraulic brakes. Henry thought mechanical brakes safer, and likely enough he was right. The V-8 would have sold better from the start if Henry had been willing to compromise with his judgment, but he was not willing when the car first appeared on March 31. He had to give in eventually, and go hydraulic in response to customer demand.

The latest "universal car" was launched on its career when business conditions were going from bad to worse, when the Brazilian government was burning millions of tons of coffee in an effort to lift prices for the remainder of the crop, when groups of unemployed marched on Washington, and the world seemed to be going to the dogs—with a revolution in Spain and civil war raging in China. Henry wore his usual untroubled smile, radiated confidence, and turned out V-8's and Model A's.

In a troubled world he was more than pulling his weight, doing his best to bring back good times.

Whether they rode in a Ford, a Chevrolet, a Plymouth, or on the subway, people admired old Henry—even those who had been the most annoyed by some of his eccentricities. In a changing world, he was the changeless optimist, still bent on service.

At a time when manufacturers couldn't sell half of what they were producing, Henry ran a public statement over his signature: "We have never yet had a sufficient production of all the things which the family needs. It would be splendid if the world should seriously attempt to overproduce everything that everybody needs. We should then discover that our present machine facilities could not even catch up with the need. Give the world a money system that makes it easier for goods to flow from man to man, and all the factories on earth could not begin to supply a tenth of the demand."

Nearly everybody agreed that he was right—for everybody wanted something that he couldn't afford to buy. But nobody could do much about it. Henry was doing more than anybody. He was building a high quality car and was selling it at a low price—from $475 to $610 for an improved V-8 in 1933. It had a 75 horse power engine, could travel 84 miles an hour, run over 18·35 miles on a gallon of petrol at normal speed.

The new V-8 had a longer wheel base, a roomier body, better upholstery, better carpet on the floor, safety glass in all windows, cowl lights, two tail lights—in case one should go out—and two horns. If one wouldn't work, the other would. You could always sound warning that another Ford was passing by.

Chapter Thirty-three

BEFORE the end of 1932, twenty-six of the thirty-two Ford assembly plants in the United States had closed. Blast furnaces and steel mills and the glass plant had closed, and production of cars dropped to four hundred thousand a year in plants whose capacity was two million cars a year.

Henry came to another decision. "No use being all worn out when the tide turns," he told reporters. "Take it easy and get ready." Henry took it easy by improving his car and reorganizing its manufacture.

Only a few rugged industrialists tried to combat the prevailing pessimism, and at the head of them was Henry, plugging sales of his car and smiling benignly. People who couldn't see a ray of light anywhere in the business world took a look at Henry's picture in the newspapers, and felt slightly better.

Roosevelt's inauguration brought a wave of optimism to the country, although the inauguration was followed by the closing of all banks, the gold embargo, and requisition of private gold holdings. Without delay Congress authorized the Chief Executive to assume temporary dictatorial power over finance and business.

The New Deal was in full swing, with executive orders following each other daily and the President making fireside chats to the citizens. Farm relief and unemployment measures tumbled out of the executive hopper, and the stock exchange was investigated—not before it needed investigating.

The National Industrial Recovery Act was passed by summer and every industry was given a code of fair practices for its guidance. The administration of American business was being taken over in a rush, amid popular enthusiasm—except for some small business men, who felt that a steamroller had passed over them. Meanwhile a score of government bureaux sprang into being to administer the codes. American industry was being regimented in a hurry, and people who didn't fall into line were said to be unpatriotic.

At the height of all this hectic enthusiasm—and a few grumbles—the automobile industry signed a code. All but Henry Ford. He didn't sign on the dotted line. And he didn't explain why he wouldn't sign. He just sat there, turning out Fords and Lincolns—he was making the Lincoln, but not paying much attention to it.

Many citizens were indignant that Ford wouldn't sign the code. There was talk of boycotting Ford cars, and organized attempts were made to make it appear that buying a Ford was a peculiarly unpatriotic thing to do.

A good many people were vocally against Henry; but, strange to relate, the sale of Ford cars suddenly increased. They were selling better than they had sold for years. It seemed that there were a lot of Americans who viewed all this enthusiastic regimentation with a slightly jaundiced eye. Evidently—and the evidence was on Ford dealers' cash registers—they were backing up Henry in a way that is peculiarly American—by spending their money for a Ford product. The government felt rather baffled—it hadn't followed Henry's career closely, nor had it studied the peculiar regard in which he was held by the average American, whom more than one administration has discovered to be largely unpredictable. Americans, like Henry Ford, are individualistic.

It gradually came out that Henry believed that the suspension of anti-trust laws and of competition was unAmerican—and Henry was nothing if not American. Henry thought that the President had a right to work things out as he deemed best, and he would do nothing to hamper the Presidential activities. But he held to the firm belief that nothing can be done by government decree. If something is to be fixed, you must fix the basic design, not pass laws about it. Henry had always fixed the design, and he was going to take his stand on that. He'd fixed things about the Model T and the Model A, and his fixing had worked. Let the government monkey around as it liked, and had a right to do. Henry also had a right to go his own way, as one lone American.

However, he believed that the law as laid down should be observed—child labour laws, minimum wages, all the rest of it. It was pointed out that not only did Ford abide by the laws —he went ahead of them in all particulars, and had been doing it for years and years. What the government demanded, he had been doing, of his own free will, for some fifteen years, and was still doing. If he didn't want to sign a code, that was his privilege—signing wasn't in the law, only compliance.

The American character of Henry's stand was evident to the American people, and threats of boycotting his products no longer were heard. Editors of magazines and newspapers implored Henry to state his views. He said nothing. He wasn't against any Presidential programme—and he just wasn't signing on the dotted line. He stood on that. And by this time the people had begun to think, and were saying to each other, "By golly! Henry may have something there! He won't be dictated to."

The American people were being dictated to; but they liked to see one American who wasn't falling into line. They bought Fords, and watched the Chevrolets go by.

By early 1934 the country was staggering up from desolation and unemployment, and people were feeling better. In January Ford sold 57,575 cars, or 25 per cent more than he had expected to sell when the year dawned. It was the best month since 1932. That month Ford spent $41,000,000 in wages and materials, and some closed assembly plants were reopened to deliver V-8's to an eager nation. By this time there were hydraulic brakes, and various refinements.

Sales in the Detroit area were three times those of any other low-priced car. Production was rising, so was Ford publicity.

In a race for stock cars at Los Angeles, twenty-two of the twenty-six entrants drove Fords, and ten finished ahead of any other make, averaging over sixty-two miles an hour for the course, which was largely curves. On a straighter course in another road race, a Ford had travelled eighty miles an hour for the distance.

Henry put on a show at the Century of Progress Exposition at Chicago, putting up a building a thousand feet long and filling it with treasures from his museum, and laying down sample roads—from dirt and cobblestones to concrete. Various exhibits showed how the products of mines and the soil were made into cars.

Meanwhile he was putting wages back to his old schedules, a general raise affecting forty-seven thousand of the seventy thousand workers in his plants. When asked why he was raising wages while car prices were down and the cost of materials was still going up, Henry replied, "When prices go up, business goes down." He intimated that he was paying too much for materials, and that if his suppliers didn't do something about it, he'd make the stuff himself. They took the hint, and did what they could to stem rising prices.

Henry wore a velvet glove of policy in such matters, but he had an iron fist inside it. If a manufacturer supplied Ford with parts, he would in time find that half or more than half of his entire output was going to Ford, his biggest customer. If Henry figured the cost of things supplied to him was too high, he'd call for a cut in price. If it wasn't forthcoming, he could make the part himself—and leave the small manufacturer with a factory and only half enough business to keep it producing at an efficient rate. Thus, Henry controlled the prices in many factories other than his own, and gradually forced prices down. The savings he passed along to the buyers of Ford cars—he didn't pocket them. Those manufacturers who most hated the procedure had to admit that Henry wasn't doing it for selfish reasons. He was simply at his old game of getting prices of things down to a point where the citizenry with a deflated pocketbook could buy.

By May 1934, the great River Rouge plant, heart of the far-flung Ford industries, was pumping the lifeblood of commerce with all its old-time energy. Production at River Rouge, and in other plants that had reopened for production, was ninety thousand cars a month. Again Henry was looking forward to a million-car year, and producing a car that had all the features of the highest-priced cars except weight, flossy upholstery, and finer finishes.

The old days, of the Model T, during its last stages, when anyone in a Ford looked transportationally efficient, but antiquated, were gone. So were the days when a little four-cylinder motor popped away in the front end of the Model A. The new V-8 was a car in which anyone might ride and feel very good about himself.

Henry, the master mind of standardization with his Model T, had himself, in turn, been standardized by the automobile industry, and by public buying preference. Again he was riding high, by his own genius and initiative. But the public, it must be confessed, had prodded him into it as far as the Model T was concerned.

Chapter Thirty-four

DEPRESSIONS might come and depressions might go, but Henry Ford, like the famous brook of the poem, ran on undisturbed, season after season, year after year.

He had done yeoman service in World War I; had survived the dislocations of peace; had led the way to a rising American prosperity during the mid-thirties and now, in 1938, was watching the war clouds gather over Europe and, as usual, was having something to say on the matter.

On September 14, 1938, he told a New York *Herald* reporter, "War is on its last legs because now it can get around and kill the fellows behind the lines, those fellows who create war. That will stop it."

He had a panacea to stop war. "They can't hide behind armies and navies any longer," he declared. "The airplanes will go over and get them. They will pay for the destruction that they are trying to bring upon the world."

Henry still hadn't caught up on his reading of history. He had said in the Chicago *Tribune* libel trial that history was bunk, and apparently he still believed it. Why should he read history, anyway? He was making history himself, and had no time for looking backward. Not even as far back as the last war.

But in a changing world, Henry Ford was soon to demonstrate his ability to change. On May 28, 1940, when he was nearing his seventy-seventh birthday, he said that as much as he hated war, "if it should become necessary the Ford Motor Company could, with the counsel of men like Lindbergh and Rickenbacker, under our own supervision and without meddling by government agencies, swing into the production of a thousand airplanes of a standard design a day. Of course, they would have to be of standardized design. Equally important would be freedom of action, so that we would not have the handicaps of red tape that slowed down production during the World War."

He said that he was convinced that the conflict in Europe, which had started in September 1939, would not last very long, "because the United States won't get into it".

"Don't misunderstand me," he said. "A lot of pressure is being brought to push us into it and there is real danger in enormous 'defensive' armament, but I am confident we can keep out of it." Henry, after all, hadn't changed a lot. He was talking pretty much as he had talked before the beginning of World War I.

It is inexplicable that a man of the genius of Henry Ford could see so dimly when he peered over the wire fences that surrounded his factories. The explanation, perhaps, lies in the fact that he had been born and had lived in a nation that had founded its fortune on the production of material things to be spread among the greatest number of people, thus to raise their standard of living and their comfort in life. Perhaps it was impossible for him to comprehend that throughout history the United States and such other nations as Canada, Australia, France, and the Scandinavian countries, had been the only ones to attempt to do much for the average citizen. Even England, a basically democratic nation despite its monarchical form of government, had kept its workmen at little above subsistence levels, while elevating the mercantile and ruling classes.

But Henry could see nothing of that—or never said that he saw it. To him, all the world, except America, may have seemed like still backward areas, gradually to be brought forward by the magic stimulus of mass production—especially of automobiles. At seventy-six, Henry still was as naïve politically as he had been when he sat in the little red schoolhouse and imbibed at the fount of learning presided over by the good McGuffey.

He was still suspicious of bankers, and in that month of May 1940, had this to say: "One of the things we must remember is that preparedness for defence is also preparedness for war and with tremendous so-called 'defensive armament', we are in just the position the warmakers want us to be in order to be pushed into a conflict in which we should have no part, pushed in by an insidious middle group that is fighting neither Germany nor England but getting them to fight each other solely that this group might profit financially. The real 'fifth column' in this country are those financial interests that make money out of war, propagate it and peddle propaganda."

Henry evidently was intimating that the powerful German nation and the great British Empire had been hurled into war by the machinations of American "financial interests" that would profit from a world holocaust. A high school sophomore should have been educated beyond such superficial reasoning. But Henry Ford had not been so well educated, he was still Henry, the intellectually barefoot boy of the little red schoolhouse. His words were not laughed at, but only because with another side of his brain he had evolved the vast Ford empire.

By June 25, 1940—after the fall of France, and when England alone faced the Nazi might—Henry Ford, the believer in democracy, announced to the National Defence Advisory Commission his "refusal to manufacture aircraft engines in the United States for the British government". That announcement forced cancellation of plans for early mass production by the Ford Motor Company of the Rolls-Royce engine, power plant of the British Hurricanes and Spitfires of the Royal Air Force which at the time were the sole defenders of democracy against the German war machine. The British Army had retreated from Dunkirk, leaving all of its war equipment behind it; England was endeavouring with desperate haste to replace that lost equipment; and under Lend-Lease, the United States Government actually was taking part in the war by supplying old reconditioned destroyers and much artillery and small arms to the British. But Henry would have no part of it. He was an isolationist.

Edsel Ford had carried on the negotiations for the Ford Motor Company to build Rolls-Royce engines. He had been made president and treasurer of the Ford Motor Company in 1918, when Henry assumed an advisory capacity, supposedly devoting his time to farming, experimenting with agriculture, the development of water power, and the collection of old Americana for his Edison Museum at Dearborn. However, he still maintained actual control of the destinies of the Ford empire, and there is no evidence that anyone ever failed to follow his advice. For that matter, whose advice had proved to be more reliable throughout the years?

There were rumours that Edsel sometimes disagreed with his father, and would argue for some point. Henry would listen with interest, but would remain unmoved if he had already made up his mind.

During the discussions about a Rolls-Royce contract with the National Defence Advisory Commission, Edsel was in Washington. Henry wasn't present. He was back in Dearborn, collecting old railroad trains for his museum. The New York *Herald Tribune* correspondent reported: "Mr. Edsel Ford requested that he be allowed to discuss this phase of the matter with Mr. Henry Ford, and the next day he called Mr. Knudsen on the telephone and said the arrangement was satisfactory."

Despite the fact that he was president of the Ford company, Edsel never made any important move without the approval of Henry. At seventy-six, Henry still kept a firm hand on all matters of policy.

That was understandable. There was something quite overpowering in the quiet personality of Henry—and all of those who worked for him in highly paid executive positions must have felt that their success, in large measure, stemmed from the success of Henry Ford. You could sense the deference in their attitude as they chatted with him.

The only people who ever seemed to meet Henry on even ground were a few newspapermen—rugged and cynical individuals, all of them—and a few old pilots—also rugged and usually irreverent characters. They would talk to Henry, ask him questions, often disagree with him—especially on aviation. Henry might simply smile and walk away without answering. But he didn't always walk away victoriously. Often he beat a retreat in silence.

It was a dignified silence, but to more than one veteran pilot it seemed curiously empty. His aeronautical activities seemed curiously amateur and fumbling. With a billion dollars, he should have done something more worth while for aviation than supplying an airport—and a mooring mast for huge, clumsy gasbags that every airplane pilot laughed at. And the years were to prove the pilots right, and Henry wrong.

Chapter Thirty-five

THE summer of 1940 was an interesting one for Henry Ford. Again he was in the limelight as a possible saviour of democracy, which was being threatened by the activities of Hitler and his supporters, then attacking England with enthusiasm and Stukas.

Henry had looked over a Curtiss P-40, flown to Dearborn by the Army, and said that it was about what he had expected. He would turn out a thousand a day when asked to do so. When asked if it was more complicated than he had anticipated, he said, "No." He was in one of his taciturn moods, and mostly he just looked.

A Ford spokesman—this was a device used by Ford when he didn't want to say something himself, but wanted to learn the reaction to what he would have said if he had deemed it advisable to say it—this Ford "spokesman" said to the Press: "The Ford company stands ready to build a motor that is better than anything on the market today. We can begin manufacture any time we get word from the government."

So far as the aviation world knew, Henry had no aeronautical engine-designing geniuses in his employ, and no motor built, and Ford pronouncements were taken a lot less seriously by the aviation people than they were by the general public. Aviators had watched Henry closely for a decade and a half, and they had observed that the only useful things that came out of the Ford plants were automobiles and tractors.

They felt that Henry was a dabbler in aviation, not a serious enthusiast. So far as building a thousand pursuit planes a day went, nobody in aviation believed that Henry could do it—not the way pursuit planes had to be built. Henry had stipulated a standardized design—which merely proved his ignorance about combat aviation. It is virtually impossible to standardize the design of a pursuit plane or a bomber and turn out thousands of exact replicas of it. The rapid progression of design in modern war aircraft precludes such a possibility.

No sooner does a plane reach a battle front than reports start coming back, pointing out the need for changes. It may be the need for additional armour plate here and there, for basic changes in the placing of gun turrets to eliminate blind spots, for a hundred and one reasons that were not evident until the machine went into action against enemy warcraft. Pursuit planes and bombers are in a constant state of flux. A few hundred may be alike. But the next few hundred will be different; they will incorporate changes dictated by combat necessity.

During the war, production of models was frozen for so many hundred planes of a series—and long before the last of them rolled off the line, changes were ordered. They were sent to reconversion centres where the changes were made. The next series incorporated these changes in the factory of origin.

This process, unavoidable though it was, meant costly delays in production and was contrary to production policies in the automobile industry. That was why, before the United States entered the war, such men as Ford stressed that for mass production of airplanes, engines, or anything else, the first consideration in getting under way was the crystallization of design and the avoidance of any changes once production had been started.

The aircraft industry, on the other hand, knew that changes in design, and continuing changes, were demanded by combat experience. So when the automobile industry spoke hopefully of turning out thousands of planes and engines, the experienced aviation manufacturers were sceptical. Each group learned from the other as the war orders started pouring out of Washington.

The automobile industry became more flexible; the aviation industry learned about real mass production. Henry Ford was to teach the airmen that he still knew a trick or two, and that it didn't matter what field you were working in if your basic principles were right.

At the World's Fair in New York in 1940, the Ford Motor Company marked its thirty-seventh anniversary by welcoming the twenty-eight millionth Ford back from a tour of the United States, Canada, and Mexico. Asked about those thousand airplanes a day, Edsel Ford said, "If the plane is commercially produceable, we can do it." He said the company could be geared for production within six months.

On the eve of his seventy-eighth birthday, July 30, 1941, Henry Ford was visualizing a new scheme of things dedicated to peace and prosperity.

"The world is learning tolerance as never before," he said, blandly ignoring events in Europe, and not even mentioning Hitler. "It is beginning to see that there is need on earth for every race."

He could look ahead and see the whole world meeting as brothers, understanding each other. From that, he said, may arise, "a federation of the whole world, because there will be more understanding". Just how far ahead that happy time might be, he didn't say. Certain elements, he intimated, would have to be eliminated. He mentioned specifically, "the munitions makers who foster and promote war". Within a few months he was to become one of the greatest munitions makers in the world himself. He was as optimistic as ever.

> What's happening right now (he declared to the Associated Press), is like the spring breaking up the winter's ice. The new world is surging up from below. And it will be filled with opportunity for everybody who can stop looking backward. Even a person 90 years old can start at scratch and make a great success—if he or she will face forward. Right now a new world is being born—a very different world.

It was indeed a different world, after Pearl Harbour. But Henry was geared for any change. In September 1941, he was handed a government contract to build nearly $300,000,000 worth of 2,000 horse power, 18-cylinder radial aircraft engines developed by the Pratt & Whitney people at East Hartford, Conn.

Henry had the order, and no factory in which to build engines without stopping production on cars. He looked at a huge concrete-paved parking place at River Rouge. "Clear the lot, and let the cars park where they can," he said. Then he ordered his materials, hired men, and got to work to set up the frame of an aircraft engine factory with a total capacity of 70,000,000 cubic feet of space enclosed by steel, concrete, and glass.

Winter came, and with it a huge fibreboard shell large enough to cover the factory that spread over 33 acres of ground. Inside this temporary, heated building, the workers built the factory —a $37,000,000 plant. As parts of the building were completed, machinery was moved in. On April 1, engineers and workers moved in. And by May 1 engines were coming off the production lines. Aviation people were amazed—old Henry had startled them again. And he was seventy-eight.

His engineers simplified the processes of mass production and applied automobile engine procedure to aircraft engine production—something now possible because of the vast volume being built. Lacking experienced workers, Henry opened an airplane apprentice school to train men at the rate of 3,000 a month.

In the spring of 1941 he had contracted with the government to build a huge bomber plant at Willow Run, thirty miles from Detroit. It was a farming area where Henry had been growing soybeans, one of his favourite farm products. Away went the beans, and up went factory buildings and hangars. The size of the area, including the airport, was 975 acres.

Four months after Pearl Harbour, Henry threw open the doors and invited the Press to inspect his latest doings. Already some 7,000 men and women were on the job making parts for the B-24 Liberator bomber and there were to be 100,000 workers eventually. And already Ford engineers were at their old task of simplifying production, of making more and more of the plane by automatic machines. Eventually they turned out over 5,000 Liberators.

With production of bombers, aircraft engines, jeeps, and Ford cars humming along, Henry Ford met reporters on his seventy-ninth birthday in 1942. He sat in his first car, built half a century before, and had his picture taken. Looking at the first car he had built, he remarked that he guessed he "must be getting on in years". But he added that he had never felt better, and his appearance confirmed his words. Except for a slight stoop of his shoulders, he was as straight as a ramrod and had neither gained nor lost any of his ten stone, a weight he had held for years.

He was host at breakfast for the newspapermen, and was his usual genial, placid self, full of optimism. He declined now to guess about the possible duration of the war, but reiterated his conviction that "nobody ever wins anything out of armed conflict". The years after the war ended were to prove him right, again.

But he could see more than a ray of light. He could see the sun beaming through the post-war clouds.

"Perhaps out of this war we may learn to think," he remarked hopefully, "and if you cause the people to think, ultimately they will think right—after they have made a lot of mistakes. That's education, and it is only through education that we can have happiness and prosperity."

He maintained that "wars never settle anything"—ignoring the fact that a war had settled the matter of American independence, for one thing, and that every nation in the course of history had been born in war, and eventually most had perished in war.

He predicted a world federation as an ultimate certainty, and denied that there was anything idealistic or impractical about it. "Intensive production means a world busy in work and a friendly and helpful exchange of goods," he declared. "Such a world has neither time nor incentive to war." That was the world, as Henry saw it from Dearborn on his seventy-ninth birthday, while all the energies of his vast industrial empire were dedicated to the destruction of much of the world then existing.

He made no mention of his war enterprises, but looked forward to freight-carrying airplanes that would go far towards solving the world's distribution policies. While his factories were making machines to distribute bombs, Henry was thinking of freight in the years of peace ahead. He was rather doubtful about the family airplane and thought it still some years away.

In the little Martha-Mary chapel in Greenfield Village, Henry was presented with a bouquet of seventy-nine roses by the children who attended school in the village. From Mrs. Ford he received a new necktie and a luggage bag.

These simple gifts seemed entirely appropriate for Henry Ford, who all his life never had wanted very much for himself, and had spent little upon himself personally.

Chapter Thirty-six

ONE day in January 1942, Edsel Ford, Henry Ford's only child, entered the Ford Hospital in Detroit to be operated on for stomach ulcers. Sixteen months later, on May 26, 1943, Edsel Ford was dead at the age of forty-nine.

His death placed upon the shoulders of his nearly eighty-year-old father the executive direction of the immense industrial empire started forty years before with an initial paid-in capital of twenty-eight thousand dollars.

Henry had able lieutenants: but again he was the active head of his vast enterprises.

For some time before the death of Edsel Ford, rumours of disintegration within the Ford top organization had been rampant. There had been many resignations of key men who had been with Ford for years.

It was rumoured in Detroit that the Ford empire was falling apart. But Henry didn't seem to be worried. He had heard such rumours before. And during the years many men had left his employ. It was said that Ford executives resembled that boy in the Indian rope trick, who climbed to the top of a rope and then disappeared. They went silently, too, for none of them ever voiced any complaint against Henry.

However, as key men left the company, others took their places, and the business went along. It was evident, however, that the cordial labour relations of the Ford company were melting away faster than the executives. Labour organizers were at work—and Henry was allergic to labour unions. Year by year, there was more and more friction between labour and the Ford management.

Henry Ford had long since become a national institution, something like the Fourth of July. His birthdays were Press events—no paper was complete on July 30 without a Ford interview. How was old Henry doing now, the world wanted to know. Henry obligingly let them know. He was going as strong as ever—at eighty.

On his eightieth birthday, the New York *Times* wrote:

Henry Ford is 80 today. Who of us has done more for the common pleasure? He is a creator. He is a great author in the sense of originator, beginner. He has made an immense fortune, the larger part of which is devoted to public use. He has given employment to multitudes. When he was born, the village, at most the county, was the limit of ordinary travel. He has enlarged for millions the scene of observation and the horizon. It is or was the fashion to snarl at machines. See what they have done for Mr. Ford and for us. . . .

He has acquired mines, forests, railways, steamships as feeders or carriers. He has been his own banker. His conception and his means of carrying it out in full may fairly be called gigantic. Though he is untainted by literature, he is a poet, a maker, an idealist. After interminable hours of work and failure after failure, the idea won. It used to be thought that he must be a crank because he insisted on paying high wages to make something that he was going to sell cheap.

He has made his mistakes and has his prejudices, but his kindliness, humanity and public spirit have long been evident. In his recent bereavement there was a strong and general public sympathy. His love of American folkways shows him in an engaging light; and the museum founded in memory of his old friend Edison is also a monument of Henry Ford's sentiment for the American past. How do you feel at 80, Mr.

Ford? "If I felt any better I would have to run." And "the main thing is to keep going", though few have gone farther than he.

At eighty Henry followed a schedule that would have tired many a man half his age. Up at five-thirty, he would walk around his estate for a while, have breakfast, leave his home at eight o'clock and be on his way to Willow Run where the Liberator bombers were moving along assembly lines. Conferences would start when he arrived and changes were discussed—there were always changes. Henry would walk miles through the shops, inspecting every major change in the huge plant. Then he'd go to River Rouge to visit the engine plant, the tractor plant and the numerous activities there. He'd lunch there, eating a frugal meal of fruit and cereal.

"Most of the sickness in the world is caused by eating too much," he told a correspondent who interviewed him for the New York *Times*. "Mixing starches and proteins is bound to cause trouble." He gave his formula for success: "Do your own work, mind your own business and don't engage in controversies. That's the way to get along. And above all else, keep away from lawyers. They are bound to get you into trouble."

He advised the reporter to read the Bible. "The Bible does not need advertising by me," he said, "but I wish more people could be persuaded to read it." He turned the pages of a small pocket Bible and read several verses having to do with thrift and the benefits of work and the evil of idleness.

He said that the world has been getting steadily better. "Nothing happens that is not for the best. One of the eternal truths of the world is that there is always change and that this change is progress. And changes occur so quickly that nobody but a fool would dare to predict what is going to happen."

On the eve of his birthday, he looked on the day not as the completion of his eightieth year, but as the beginning of his eighty-first. "And a lot of work lies ahead of me," he said with his usual confident smile. Truly, in all the world there was nobody remotely like Henry Ford.

Even newspapermen, notoriously cynical and disillusioned about nearly everything, were now taking Henry Ford as they took the Statue of Liberty—as something immovable, holding up the torch of hope. People who read these accounts, in the midst of a war, somehow felt cheered. "Good old Henry!" they'd say. "He's still going strong!" He certainly was.

By the end of the year even those cagey old aviation engineers and production men, who had said that Henry was talking through his hat when he had spoken optimistically about the production of a thousand pursuit planes a day, had to admit that he had a sound basis for his statement.

During 1943 more than one thousand big bombers had been flown away from Willow Run, and a multitude of parts had gone off for assembly elsewhere. There had been difficult engineering and man-power problems, but Henry and the efficient Ford organization had solved them.

In March 1944, in a copyrighted interview in the Atlanta *Constitution*, Ford said, "Go to work. That's the answer to everything. Laziness and idleness are the cause of all the world's troubles. By idleness I mean idle land, as well as idle people. There are millions of idle acres in the world. The way I see it, greeds, creeds and boundary lines must go."

He was looking forward to peace, yearning for the time when the huge war contracts would be cancelled, when the factories would be back on peacetime work. None of his vast war production had been used to make men happier; it had been used only for destruction. It was waste, and Henry never saw it in any other light.

He warned against a depression after the war. "There can and should be a peacetime use for all the factories built for war production. None of them need be idle and there need be no idleness anywhere after the war. I think there will be a job in the factory or on the farm for everybody who wants to work. The unhappiest man on earth is the one who has nothing to do."

He harked back to the formative period of his youth. "One of the truly important things is to put greater emphasis upon education. We should try to teach our young folks to be kind to all you chance to meet; in the field, or lane, or crowded street. Hatreds and suspicions are rampant; it's going to be a tremendous education based upon truth. You know, no matter how hard you try, you can't get away with a lie very long."

He recalled that he had built seven churches in connection with educational projects. They are run on a non-sectarian basis and some are used as schools. He suggested that churches that stand idle most of the week could be used as schools.

"If we could get all religions together on a common purpose," he said, "the elimination of jealousies and the things that make men covet another man's belongings, we would be a long way towards the goal of outmoding war, depression and poverty."

On September 21, 1945, Henry Ford for the second time resigned the presidency of the great automotive empire that he had founded in 1903. Henry Ford II, then twenty-eight years of age, succeeded his famous grandfather as president of the company and head of one of the world's greatest private fortunes.

In his letter of resignation, Mr. Ford said, "I feel free to take this step at this time because the critical period during which I again assumed office has passed. I shall be glad to remain on the board and to assist in an advisory capacity."

It had been more than sixty years since he completed the original Ford engine, the basis of a one-family empire that he had maintained against rugged competition through two world wars, through periods of depression and business uncertainty, and against any interference from banking interests.

Now he was stepping down, not because he was physically tired, but because, he explained, "I have many personal interests to which I now desire to devote most of my time."

Not the least of those interests was to watch his grandson and namesake assume responsibility, and to guide him in the great task that faced him.

Chapter Thirty-seven

DEARBORN, Henry's old home and real centre of the Ford empire, is a show place, a perpetual world's fair of exhibitions of progress in engineering, mechanics, and the useful arts. This is the Edison Institute, the combined Edison Museum and the Greenfield Village—a group of buildings which are exact reproductions of Independence Hall, Congress Hall, the old City Hall of Philadelphia, and the Dearborn Inn, a modernized New England hotel and dozens of others. There is a theatre and classrooms used by the school for children living near by. The Edison Museum is in the rear of this line of buildings.

The floor area of this huge building is 800 by 440 feet, and it is packed with the treasures that Henry Ford collected for two decades, from a locomotive of 1850 to the great generator that supplied power for the Highland Park plant before it was abandoned for River Rouge. The history of steam and petrol power is there in hundreds of ancient engines and automobiles, all of which have been reconditioned in Ford shops, and many of which can be run under their own power.

It is a museum of science, an education in the arts and crafts, from the earliest hand loom to modern weaving machines. There are ancient spinning wheels and flat irons and ruffle irons; pianos of all kinds; furniture of all periods; whole streets of stores, exact replicas of those of the 1850's. There are shops of tinsmiths, gunsmiths, potters, harness makers and dozens of others. The automobiles are of all makes and all ages; bicycles from the nineties; even the Mercedes car which the Kaiser used in World War I.

There is a reproduction of the *Rocket*, the first steam locomotive, built in England in 1829. The Ford reproduction was built from the original drawings. There is a train of cars and the Sam Hill locomotive, just such a train as that in which Edison worked as a boy, selling newspapers, magazines, and candy.

The collection of horse-drawn vehicles includes the three-wheeled phaeton in which Lafayette rode, a sleigh that carried George Washington. There are coaches, shays, barouches, victorias, omnibuses, buckboards, farm wagons, two-wheeled racing gigs, and vehicles from all over the world.

In the agricultural section, every kind of farm equipment is on view, from modern tractors back to the most primitive farming tools. The blacksmith shop of Caleb Taft, built in 1830, has been reproduced. Ford brought its entire equipment from Uxbridge, Mass. There are bellows, forges, and blacksmiths' tools, just as they were when the poet Longfellow saw them when he went to visit the blacksmith.

In the Greenfield Village are reproduced the features of village life in America a century ago. There is the Clinton Inn, built in 1831, at Clinton, Michigan, a stopping place for stagecoaches between Detroit and Chicago. Henry had it moved to Dearborn and had it furnished just as it was in its prime. The original schoolhouse in which Henry studied as a boy is there, with replicas of its desks and equipment. So is the Lincoln courthouse, brought from Logan County, Ill.

The Menlo Park buildings in which Thomas A. Edison worked to perfect his inventions are reproductions of the buildings of 1876 to 1886—and parts are from the original structures. Much of the great inventor's equipment has been gathered there, including the telegraph table at which Edison sat and sent messages to friends before the telephone was invented. The arm-chair used by him is there, too, the chair from which he watched the final tests of his incandescent lamp on October 21, 1879.

Along the village streets are Luther Burbank's office, brought from his experimental farm in California; the restored farmhouse of Edison's father; the Cotswolds Cottage group, two centuries old, imported from England and reconstructed to depict the life of two centuries ago. There are old houses and stores and the little post office brought from Greenfield, Connecticut; a shoemaker's shop built in 1828, a house from Plymouth, Michigan, built in 1845, and a cooperage shop built in 1785. There are an ancient foundry, a stone burr gristmill, a hundred-year-old sawmill, an old glass plant, and many others.

The Greenfield Village was opened to the public on June 13, 1933. Visitors were taken around in horse-drawn vehicles, as they still are, for no motor-car is allowed to enter the gates. Everything about the village must be kept just as it would have been a century or so ago—with the exception of the roads, some of which are hard-surfaced.

Henry Ford spent uncounted millions collecting the relics of the old age that he, more than any other man, had laboured to destroy. He had a sentimental interest in old things, and would spend hours wandering among his treasures, running the old engines or automobiles whenever he had a mind to. Often he would visit his old brick workshop and look at his first car; and he had an especial affection for the souvenirs of his friend Edison. It was as though he wanted to relive the days of his youth, to rest his mind from the responsibilities of his industrial empire.

To his fellow citizens he has left an enduring monument to remind them of their country's past. And that, in its way, seems to be a service as valuable as his contribution of the "universal car".

It is apparent throughout Henry Ford's life that he has been an idealist, and that faith has been the basis of his career—faith in work, in men, in service. One day when he said that faith was what the world needed, he explained what he meant by faith. "Just faith in yourself and faith that other men are trying to do the right thing, and faith that the world is run on the right principle and getting better all the time.

"People are all right," he said. "There is good in every man. I believe in all men."

Early in life he learned that thinking about money didn't carry one far, and wealth had never been of primary importance to him. "What do I want with more money?" he asked twenty years ago. "I shall never use what I have, most likely. . . . Money doesn't do me any good. I can't spend it on myself. Money has no value, anyway. It is merely a transmitter, like electricity. I try to keep it moving as fast as I can for the best interests of everybody concerned."

That he evolved an industrial empire estimated to be worth more than three-quarters of a billion dollars, owned solely by himself, his wife, his son Edsel, and Edsel's four children, might suggest that he had served himself at least as well as he had served his fellow men. Surely he was entitled to do so. Yet there is no reason to doubt that he considered himself to be no more than the trustee of this vast fortune, which he thought of, not as personal wealth, but as machinery for production of transportation for all the people. At any time during the last two decades, he could have sold his immense business to the public, could have turned it into perhaps as much as a billion dollars in cash, and could have lived in luxury and idleness on no more than a fraction of the yearly interest.

Yet he worked until almost the last. And even his resignation as president of the Ford Motor Company was dictated less by his great age and growing weakness than by the desire to see his grandson take over the management and go on to new ways of doing things, new ways of providing service to his fellow men.

Twenty years ago he had said, "Every generation has its own problems; it ought to find out its own solutions. There is no use in our living if we can't do things better than our fathers did."

Perhaps that also was in his mind when, at the age of eighty-two, he stepped aside to let his only son's eldest son, Henry Ford II, take control. Thereafter he was content to sit on the side lines, watching that able grandson initiate new policies that, for one thing at least, bettered the labour relations of the Ford company, which, in late years, had become increasingly unhappy.

The spring of 1947 brought floods to many parts of the

nation, including Dearborn County. On Monday, April 7, high flood waters of the Rouge River running through the Ford estate had cut electrical power and heating service at the residence. Henry Ford had spent a vigorous day inspecting flood water damage around the Ford plant and the estate. He never had appeared in better health, and was planning to continue his inspection on the morrow.

When he retired that night at nine o'clock, the conditions may have reminded him of his boyhood days. A wood-burning fireplace warmed the room, which was lighted only by a kerosene lamp and candles. Even the telephone had been cut off by the flood waters; and the Ford mansion may have seemed as isolated as the old farmhouse where Henry Ford had been born nearly eighty-four years before. In these surroundings, reminiscent of his boyhood, Henry Ford dropped off to sleep.

He awakened at eleven-fifteen that night, and told his wife that he felt slightly ill. Mrs. Ford gave him a drink of water. Twenty-five minutes later, in the form of a cerebral haemorrhage, death came to Henry.

Chapter Thirty-eight

HENRY FORD left the world believing that he would return. Always against waste in any form, he simply could not believe that human experience could be wasted. Life was like the scrap metal in his factories; it could be reincarnated to function again. Such was his idea—and it is no more eccentric than many of the ideas he harboured at times during his nearly eighty-four years.

Undoubtedly he was a genius, and an eccentric one. It may be said that he invented nothing, but he adapted everything that led to mass production, and his adaptations, all of them, indicated an unerring faculty for picking the right tool to perform the job.

He got his production line from the moving conveyers of the meat packers, his standardization of parts from the interchangeable parts of the gunmaker, Eli Whitney. His independence led him to buy out, one after another, the men who had been his early partners. He had to go it alone, brooking no interference from men less knowing than he in his own field of standardization and mass production.

If he had been a better-informed man, culturally, he might

have been likened to the lone eagle. Rather, he was a lone sparrow, with the sparrow's eye for tiny things—not a thing in his vast empire escaped his birdlike glance. His movements, even, were spry and birdlike, even when he had grown old.

In his world of metals, of materials, Ford was highly intelligent. In the broader world of human and national relations, he never displayed any indication that he could make connections. He could examine a watch, and see how it went together. How the world and the people in it went together, he never seemed to understand—as his pacifist stand on war demonstrated clearly.

Although he was a pacifist, he, more than any other man, made possible the total war of industrial regimentation, of mass production for destruction. There is no indication in his various public utterances that he understood this, or even sensed the part he had played.

If he had died twenty-five years ago, he would have been remembered as the apotheosis of the American dream—the poor boy who had risen triumphantly to great financial success. He would have been the one man who had a formula for banishing poverty—and if he had died in time, nobody would have known that he could not have gone on and achieved worldwide prosperity for everyone, even the Chinese coolie and the lower-depth hordes of India. As it turned out, his own empire, during his lifetime, was to experience a great recession from prosperity.

He reached the height of his career by 1925, and was already on the downgrade when, in 1927, he turned out the fifteen millionth Ford Model T. True, he made a sudden about-face, spent a hundred million dollars, scrapped thirty thousand tools —and started all over again, following the lead of General Motors.

The father of standardization and mass production had been told bluntly that there was a saturation point in everything— even mass production. He was never the same after that lesson. When he turned out the Model A, and later on the V-8, he was not taking the lead. He was following a public trend, catering to it. In 1926 he had been selling 41 per cent of the cars produced in America. By 1941 his percentage had dwindled to only 16 per cent. In 1946—due largely to the management of Henry

Ford II and his understanding of labour problems—it was back to 22 per cent.

Henry Ford, the man who had done the most for American workmen, had failed to keep up with the times, and had alienated his own workers, as far back as 1932. An autocrat at heart—despite his democratic bearing, his friendly mixing with the most humble—he had wanted to run his business his own way, without any interference from the men who worked for him. He would be good to them, but only as far as he thought he should go. The workers, who built the car, thought otherwise. There were strikes and riots at Ford plants.

Henry hired Harry Bennett, a tough, hard-faced and hard-thinking former Navy man, to head his factory police. In riots outside the Ford plant in 1932, four jobless Ford workers were killed. Thereafter Henry never went anywhere without a police guard. The friend of the working men had to protect himself against them. Ford's labour relations declined steadily until 1941, when Ford gave in and signed a union shop contract. He could have done so years before, could have saved himself loss. But he would not be dictated to—until, at last, he recognized that labour's share in industrial management had become inevitable.

Even at the height of the labour disputes, few believed that Henry Ford was being grasping, was trying to hang on to a greater share of the profits for himself. Money probably didn't enter into it, to any great extent. It was simply that Henry wouldn't let anybody share the responsibility of management. He wanted things his own way. And he got his own way, almost to the end.

Looking back on his life, it seems fair to say that Henry Ford was a man of good will; but a stubborn and self-opinionated one, highly intelligent in his own field, notably limited in others. When he looked over the fences surrounding his factories, he saw dimly. He misjudged the Jews—and honourably admitted it after six years!—he thought labour was only labour, not independent American citizens, like himself. He thought Americans wanted a cheap car—when they wanted a better-looking car, even if it cost twice as much. He thought he could stop war—with a group of crackpots and a chartered liner.

And, at the end, he believed that he was coming back! Let us hope that he is. He left the world better—and worse!—than he found it. On his next visit he may make it neither better nor worse. But at least, on his past record we may believe that he will afford it yet another interesting experience. If some amazing character pops up, any time during the next few decades, can anyone declare with certainty that it is not another Ford going by?

Chapter Thirty-nine

THE brief account given at the end of Chapter Seventeen of how the Ford car made its first impact on England, and of how an important part of Henry Ford's business was eventually established there deserves amplification into a chapter of its own.

There seems to be some doubt as to whether it was in 1903 or 1904 that the "very first ever" Ford was seen in this country. (This, of course, was not the fabulous Model T which did not make its appearance until 1909.)

Whether the actual debut of the Ford car here was in 1903 or 1904 doesn't now matter much; it was not until the Scottish Reliability Trials of 1905 in which a Ford (Model C) performed extremely well that any real notice was taken of the invader.

By this time the Central Motor Car Company had been already formed with P. L. D. Perry (now Lord Perry) as its moving spirit. This company imported and sold Model A Fords only; two years later a fresh company was formed, but it was not until 1909 that any really significant step forward was made in this country when an *English branch* of the Ford business was opened and the Model T was introduced to the English market.

At that time, of course, every nut and bolt of every Ford sold here was first made in America and the cars shipped complete to England. In that first year over four hundred Model T's were sold in England.

I have called Model T "fabulous" and I think it almost deserves that overworked epithet. It persisted, essentially unchanged, for nineteen years (from 1909 to 1927) and in that period more than fifteen million examples of it were made!

It is amusing to reflect that it almost certainly owes its somewhat odd appearance to the fact that Henry Ford was a farmer's son and had bred in his bones an appreciation of a farmer's difficulties. One result of this was that when Henry designed a car he designed one that wouldn't give any trouble in the matter of road clearance; and if, in time, this old-fashioned aspect of the Tin Lizzie provided material for a number of music-hall jokes, why should Henry mind? After all, he had sold fifteen million of the things!

During the years 1909–11 the prestige and sale of Fords were both steadily growing in England and it began to be clear that managerial changes would have to be made to keep pace with events.

Accordingly in 1911 yet another company was formed and this time it was called "Ford Motor Company (England) Ltd.". Under that title it set up business at Manchester where in fact it remained until 1928.

The business carried on at Manchester was still purely an assembly one in those days, and it gives one a shock of surprise and admiration to reflect that things have now changed to such a degree that at the present moment no fewer than eighteen countries have assembly plants in which parts made entirely in England and exported from here are built up into Ford cars!

Through the next decade and more the Manchester plant gradually changed its nature from a mere assembling unit to a constructional one, until in 1924 (to look ahead for a moment) 92 per cent of each car was actually made in this country and only 8 per cent of it imported from America.

From the beginning, of course, Henry's basic principle of "flow production" had been put into operation in the English works; indeed without it there would have been no celebration of the completion of the 250,000th British-built Ford, which happy, and significant, event took place in 1925.

But at that very same time Henry was planning to shut up the Manchester plant and to substitute for it the biggest and most advanced motor factory in Europe.

Many possible alternative sites must have been considered before a choice was made; and probably when a "short list" was arrived at there were two or three candidates for selection with very little between them and very little to sway the verdict "for" or "against".

In point of fact the choice ultimately fell on Dagenham, at that time hardly more than a village; as yet unspoilt, and undeveloped, by industry.

When one recalls that some 22,000 enormous piles had to be

driven into the marshy ground there to reinforce it before the factory could be built it is easy to believe that there were not lacking critics of the new site.

By this time in life, and indeed long before this time, Henry Ford had arrived at three basic principles on which his business was founded. Whether he ever actually put them down in writing I don't know; but it would have been easy to do so for they can be expressed on half a sheet of notepaper.

Henry Ford's three cardinal rules were these:

(1) Bring the work to the workman—don't make the man walk about after his job.

(2) Supply service after sales—don't have any dissatisfied customers.

(3) Put your factory near deep water—don't have the trouble and cost of *road-rail-sea-road-rail* transport to get the goods to your market.

All three of these principles are taken fully into account at Dagenham; but the one that hits the eye most forcibly at first is the one concerning deep-water facilities.

Dagenham lies on the tidal Thames, the waterway which for a thousand years has been the great communal highway and artery of England's trade.

Into that river Ford's factory pokes the longest privately owned wharf that the Thames knows, a jetty 1,800 feet in length at which ocean-going ships of ten thousand tons capacity can tie up. They dock in never-ending succession, bringing the coal, the iron ore, and the other basic materials which the factory will convert into vehicles and tractors at the rate of about 1,500 each working day.

This jetty, a familiar and famous sight among all who habitually use London's river, is semi-circular in shape and serves two functions: first to receive the raw materials for the job which the monster factory behind it will transform into motor vehicles, and second to load these finished vehicles neatly boxed into vessels waiting to take them literally all over the world; and it is a remarkable sight to stand in the middle of the wharf and to see these two activities, the alpha and omega of the complex thing, being carried on, one on your right hand, the other on your left.

By the time the move to Dagenham was made the Fordson tractor was already a very considerable part of the production programme.

A motorist who attempts to get from London to Brighton on a fine Sunday in the summer may sometimes have doubts whether continuous production of cars rolling off the assembly lines is an unmixed blessing; but the human being who has ever been to China, to India, to Russia, to Australia and has seen in these countries the vast areas of untilled land, can have no doubts at all about the value, indeed about the completely vital necessity of tractor production.

The truth is that whereas man allows his own numbers to increase each year, each day, each hour with startling rapidity and that increase has been going on for centuries, he had done virtually nothing until forty years ago to increase the rate at which he was providing food for himself.

The rate of ploughing a field was no greater in 1910 than it was in 910.

Had no means been found of altering this state of things it is quite likely that the German submarine warfare of 1914–18 would have proved decisive and this country might well have been forced to surrender through starvation.

Henry Ford met, as we have already seen, the urgent request of the British government for help, and in 1917 a Fordson tractor ploughed its first furrow in English soil.

Largely as a result of the impetus of that initial step taken under the spur of compulsion, agriculture in these islands is now more highly mechanized than anywhere else in the world.

Dagenham assists in this vital business of giving man the tools to grow more food for his ever-increasing family by turning out one completed Fordson tractor every three or four minutes of each working day.

Stated baldly like that in print it doesn't sound likely, in fact it doesn't sound possible; but the fact is there: if you stand at the end of the tractor assembly lines you can see them rolling off, and on the blackboard at the side you can read the tally as it is kept during the day: 18 for the first hour, 17 for the next (tea interval!), 19 for the next, and so on.

It may be imagined that to move house from Manchester to Dagenham was an undertaking of magnitude. Many of the men already employed at the Manchester plant went south with the works, and today in Dagenham among the forty thousand or so people employed there you can still hear an occasional Lancashire accent.

Visually the most impressive thing about the huge aggregation of buildings at Dagenham is probably the power house.

It looks striking enough as you see it from the river front, but when you get inside it is impossible not to feel something of the majesty of sheer power.

The immense building with its lofty glass roof, its spotlessly clean floor, its bewildering array of multi-coloured pipes seems like some cathedral of man's New Religion; and all the time as you stand there looking about you, you feel the whole place, the very floor beneath your feet, throbbing and pulsating with *power*.

This is the heart of all the huge concern that lies immediately outside, a concern outside whose principal offices there rightly stands a statue of Henry Ford.

There he stands, a slim and in many ways a not very impressive figure; and if it were the man himself in person who could speak he would surely approve of what he sees, for Dagenham as it is today exemplifies pretty well all that Henry Ford stood for and believed in.

Henry liked to control all (or at any rate as much as possible) of the business of making his cars, and Dagenham is virtually a self-contained factory.

As we have seen, the raw materials come there in their most primitive state: coal, iron ore, limestone.

Dagenham deals with these things in its own blast furnace (the only one in the south of England) and converts them to its own uses.

Henry believed in bringing the job to the man; and in making machines do as much of the work as possible.

He would have approved, then, of the rather more than eight thousand machine tools packed incredibly close together and of the miles of conveyor belt and track which run continuously through the factory.

Henry believed passionately in supplying service for each car that he sold, so he would surely give his blessing to the two hundred tons of spare parts which leave daily for the service stations.

Henry liked to dream of the cars and the tractors that he made going out all over the world, and Dagenham would please him there, too, for it is now the largest motor exporting factory in the world, and more vehicles are exported from here than from all other Ford factories combined!

Henry believed, as we know, in deep-water facilities; and here all day long he can hear the swish of the tidal Thames close behind him and the hooting of steamers, cargo-loaded, Ford-loaded, setting out for the ends of the earth.

Yes, Henry Ford, that dynamic and shrewd, yet in some ways extremely simple man would surely be pleased with his British offspring which is striving so vigorously and so successfully, to prove he was right when he said: "If everybody in the world gets a chance of buying what he wants there won't ever be enough machines to make the goods."

Index